# THE ALMOST CHURCH *Revitalized*

OTHER BOOKS BY MICHAEL DURALL

*Creating Congregations of Generous People*

*Beyond the Collection Plate*

*The Almost Church*

*Living A Call: Ministers and Congregations Together*

# THE ALMOST CHURCH *Revitalized*

## Envisioning the Future of Unitarian Universalism

Michael Durall

CommonWealth

MICHAEL DURALL
The Almost Church Revitalized:
Envisioning the Future of Unitarian Universalism

Published by CommonWealth Consulting Group
1465 Sierra Drive
Boulder, CO 80302
www.vitalcongregations.com



ISBN 978-1-60743-838-0

Printed in the United States of America

CONTENTS

To the many UU clergy, lay leaders, and people in the pews
who shared their hopes and dreams with me.
You made this book possible, and I am very grateful.

*We don't have to be as we are. This is good news indeed.*
*We are not trapped in our histories or our fears.*
*We can set ourselves, and our communities, on a new course.*

*While this good news is liberating, it is also unnerving,*
*destabilizing, even frightening. But we cannot rely on things*
*always being the way they are.*

— Stephanie A. Paulsell, Harvard Divinity School

*However sheltered this port, and however calm these waters,*
*we must not anchor here.*

— Walt Whitman

# Introduction

This is an uplifting book. Most readers of *The Almost Church* found my challenges to Unitarian Universalism's sacred cows engaging and thought-provoking. But others felt I was negative, not offering suggestions about how to do things better. This book contains scores of ideas that will help UU congregations become more influential in their communities and more effective in achieving their hopes and dreams.

*The Almost Church Revitalized* is all new, not a reworking of the previous edition. Its purpose is to bring readers an enlightened glimpse of congregational life today, from our own tradition and from other faiths, as well. UUs may differ with other denominations theologically, but churches of many faiths are extraordinarily progressive and offer much to be learned.

This is also a realistic book. Back in the 1950s, most people went to church, at least on Sunday. Those who didn't felt they probably should. Most Americans held a positive view of the traditional church. Before the interstate highway system created a mobile American society, many churches presented a Norman Rockwell portrait, with three generations of families in the pews, wearing their Sunday best. That era is long gone.

Today, in church terms, the fastest-growing segment of the population is the un-churched. Only about two percent of congregations nationwide, of all faiths, have grown by five percent or more over the past few years.[1] In Unitarian Universalism, this means fewer than 100 congregations have seen meaningful growth, while the remaining 950 have experienced membership plateaus or have gone into decline. I'm not being negative. I'm just the messenger.

Established churches today face two cultural groups of people. The first group, born before about 1955, came of age in the disappearing world of the traditional, respected church. The second group includes younger generations born into the emerging non-church world. If young people have an interest in religion at all, it's likely to be in a church of their same-age peers, or they view private spirituality as more appealing than the institutional church.[2] And there's the rub. The methods used by established churches to reach younger generations fall on the deaf ears of those raised in an un-churched culture.

What's a congregation to do? If established churches adapt their methods to reach young people (for instance, contemporary music) this may cause distress among older generations. This is not to say that young people alone are Unitarian Universalism's salvation. But traditional churchgoers today live in a rapidly changing society that is increasingly indifferent to religious expression. This altered environment calls for a far-reaching new perspective if Unitarian Universalism is to maintain its place on the American religious landscape. Time is not on our side, and gradualism will not do. Systemic change needs to occur in the very short term.

In this book, I make the case that many of Unitarian Universalism's most valued traditions are in actuality its greatest liabilities. UU churches build on many strengths. But a hopeful tomorrow will require discarding a sizable number of practices that have outlived their usefulness. This is a significant challenge.

But I also contend that countless alternatives exist. Many are extremely attractive and offer hope for the future. Throughout this book, we'll take a look at how UU congregations can evolve to meet the challenges of a new tomorrow.

Readers may rest assured that the alternatives I present do not include a rock and roll music, wave-your-arms-in-the-pews, video screen church that is popular today. In his book, *Who Stole My Church?* Gordon MacDonald writes compellingly about the loss that parishioners suffer when new leadership transforms the church into something they no longer recognize.[3]

My intention in writing this book is to help clergy, lay leaders, and people in the pews understand more fully the nature and character of their congregations. In doing so, I hope they will become more adventurous, mischievous, and successful in their roles.

Michael Durall
Boulder, Colorado
February, 2009

CHAPTER 1

# A Public or a Private Church?

*"We have been buffeted by private spiritualities that have no connection to public life."*
— *Sojourner Magazine* Editor Jim Wallis[1]

I recently attended the opening of a community health clinic, funded almost entirely by a local church. This church had received a bequest from a long-term member, whose only desire was that the money be used for the greater good. The congregation believed how it spent this money would reveal the church's true nature and character, so they raised an equal amount and built the health clinic in a marginal neighborhood. It just didn't seem right to put all that money in the bank, for the congregation's use alone.

Many churches throughout the United States have funded large-scale community projects. Asylum Hill Congregational Church in Hartford, CT, is an excellent example. This congregation raised over $1 million from its members, pulled some strings around town, and built a Boys and Girls Club a few blocks down the street.

A layperson who spoke at the health clinic's opening said she was proud to be part of a "public" church. She conveyed the dedication of that congregation to its primary purpose — to serve the public good. There was hardly a dry eye in the crowd. This congregation held great appeal for me. It had a distinct purpose. The church's theology, different from my own, mattered little.

I don't know of any UU church that has constructed a project on the scale of a community health clinic or a Boys and Girls Club, though many have the financial resources to do so. (The UU Church of Ottawa, Canada, has a low-income housing facility on its grounds, but this project was government funded.)

While most UU congregations are involved in smaller-scale initiatives, I don't believe Unitarian Universalism can claim the status of a "public" church, that the greater good is its primary purpose. Does that mean Unitarian Universalism is some type of private church? I don't wish to debate the semantics of the words public and private, and perhaps "private church" is not an exact descriptor. But the concept warrants consideration.

William Murry, UU minister and former president of Meadville Lombard Theological School in Chicago, addressed this very issue. He said, in part:

> *Too often we have understood our task as relegated to the private sphere, the personal lives of our members. Too often we have preached sermons on trivial and inconsequential subjects rather than address the significant issues of our times. In a word, too many of our ministers and churches have retreated into the safety and security of the private sphere and have little or no public ministry, and that is tragic.*[2]

I believe Murry's prophetic words have a direct bearing on how UU congregations view their role in the world, and whether or not they will grow in membership.

## Searching for Truth

William Murry's phrase, "private sphere" is an excellent example of a perceived UU strength that in actuality is a weakness. The UUA principle of "A free and responsible search for truth and meaning," is of questionable value, and may be detrimental to future growth. This is because the search for truth is the quintessential private spirituality.

Perhaps I am biased, but searching for truth strikes me as an enigma. In Catholic high school, a priest encouraged me to meditate on the mysteries of the Holy Rosary. Decades later, I've yet to conjure up a single mystery. My inner search for truth has been equally elusive.

My skepticism includes wondering how large a supply of truth actually exists. Science-oriented UUs may ponder what tools are used to measure truth. Or, might we find truth in a certain time period, like a fiscal year? And what do we do with truth once we have found it? Do people reach a certain capacity for truth, that they eventually possess enough, or is one's capacity limitless?

When I witnessed the ribbon-cutting ceremony opening that health center, the search for truth struck me as trifling in comparison to what this congregation had accomplished. This church had brought about a miracle. Thousands of lives would be made better. The personal search for truth resounded not only as trivial, but indifferent to a world in great need.

### The Private Church

This brings us back to the concept of the "private" church. Perhaps that phrase isn't entirely precise. But Murry's notion of the "private sphere" resonates accurately. The future growth of Unitarian Universalism may hinge on this very concept.

America now sports a multimillion-dollar "spirituality" business. Countless opportunities exist to seek truth via books, DVD's, seminars, conferences, and residential retreats. Many are based on Eastern faiths and offer people the opportunity to delve deeply within themselves. Others have a more questionable basis and are prosperity oriented, teaching subjects like, "Nine Spiritual Practices for Getting Everything You Want."

My purpose is not to rate these programs, but rather to say they attract people who are on the inner search for truth. While spirituality-related programs have flourished, their success has not translated into increased attendance at traditional churches.

If UU congregations and the denomination itself emphasize the search for truth as a fundamental goal, they are attempting to reach this segment of the population. At this writing, the UUA's home page on its website emphasizes the search for truth. But people on the search for truth are unlikely to believe they will find what they're seeking in organized religion. (Jokes about being a disorganized religion are amusing, but not helpful.) Beyond this particular segment of the population, the search for truth is not a motivating factor for the vast majority of church shoppers today.

We needn't completely abandon the search for religious truth, or the belief that revelation is not sealed. But these should be a secondary focus, at best. Our primary concern should lie elsewhere — away from the private sphere to becoming a public church, one that reaches out to create a more just and humane world. UUs are among the most highly educated and affluent of American churchgoers, and such a goal is well within their reach.

You can perform a simple test to determine the extent to which your congregation takes a public or private stance. Just look for the "outreach" or "social action" line item in the church's budget. This line item is separate from denominational or district dues. Protestant congregations, churchgoers most like UUs in socioeconomic terms, maintain a budget line item for outreach of between 10 and 29 percent, with the national average being 16 percent. This money goes to people who are less fortunate, beyond the church's four walls. These are churches whose primary orientation is outward, toward the community.

If the line item in your congregation's budget is appreciably less, or nonexistent, this indicates an inwardly focused congregation. Most likely, the emphasis is on maintenance and a principal concern for members who are already there. This is a congregation that essentially gives money to itself, a private church. Such a situation should be a matter of conscience for UUs of good faith.

If UU congregations wish to engage the world in more meaningful ways, they will need to become more outward oriented, public churches that challenge members to reach new segments of the population with a very different message. That is the subject of the next chapter.

CHAPTER 2

# Why Unitarian Universalism Has Not Grown and How to Turn That Around

*The problem is that it's a self-populating institution. Knowledge is institutionalized. Those involved aren't able to evaluate their own systems. They don't have the mechanisms to get rid of what doesn't work anymore.*

— Michael Lewis, from his book *Moneyball*, about how a radical new approach taken by the Oakland A's baseball team allows it to win more games than teams with higher payrolls

*A focus on attracting individuals reinforces continuity and tends to attract replacements for departing members. It may or may not result in modest numerical growth.*

— Church author Lyle Schaller

Lyle Schaller, the author of 40 books about congregational life, introduced a revolutionary concept in church growth a number of years ago. This is an idea whose time has come. Rather than hoping individuals or families show up at random, Schaller believes that congregations should reach out and engage groups of people, or cohorts of the population.[1]

This concept is radically different from how UU and Protestant congregations attempt to grow in membership. It holds great promise for the future. It is the ideal antidote to the attitude, "If people are lucky they'll find us; but if not, there isn't much we can do about that, is there?"

Before outlining Schaller's approach, we need to consider an unvarnished account of why Unitarian Universalism has not grown in membership for almost 50 years. My intent is not to dwell on shortcomings in the movement. Rather, it is necessary to identify systemic weaknesses in order to contemplate the far-reaching changes necessary if Unitarian Universalism is to grow in membership and thrive in the years to come.

Some readers may be thinking, "Why do we have to grow? I like my congregation the way it is now." Admittedly, many UUs are satisfied with their congregation's current size. However, church members move away and pass away, and congregations need to grow by five to ten percent each year to maintain current membership levels. Also, UU congregations are living, breathing entities. They are not petrified forests, forever locked in time. If churches do not achieve some amount of consistent growth, they will lose their ability to do so, and eventually dwindle. Perhaps close their doors. No one wants this.

The description of Unitarian Universalism to follow is remarkably similar to liberal Protestantism. Denominations like the Lutherans, Methodists, Presbyterians, and Episcopalians have lost millions of members over the past few decades, for the very reasons enumerated below. But take heart. For every shortcoming, I propose an alternative.

## The global view of why UU congregations have not grown

The most straightforward way to convey why Unitarian Universalism has not grown is to employ a marketing concept. Most UU churches are unwilling and possibly unable to "redefine the product." The product in question is a church of today that is comparable to that of decades past. UU congregations have not remained competitive. They have not evolved to adapt to a rapidly changing environment, one that is increasingly unsympathetic to religious expression. Like major league baseball mentioned in the opening quote, UU congregations have been unable to jettison what no longer works.

I visit churches of many denominations frequently. I often come away feeling that I've traveled back in time. The Order of Service, music, readings, announcements, and worship elements are strikingly similar to the 1950s. I also experience a sense of déjà vu, that I'm visiting the same church over and over. The church appears to be locked in time, trapped in the past.

This occurs for three reasons. First, most UU congregations fall into the "family" or "pastoral" category, which means fewer than 100 to 125 people attend Sunday services. For church members of many faiths, this is the ideal congregational size. Congregants see their friends on Sunday morning and life is relatively uncomplicated. Numerical growth is not a priority and may rarely be discussed. Small congregations sometimes resemble small towns, where outsiders are viewed with suspicion. Small churches often appear impenetrable to newcomers.

If smaller congregations can attract five or ten new members each year to replace the five or ten who move on, the church will retain its equilibrium. The only hitch is that smaller congregations tend to be growing older and grayer. They are unlikely to attract younger generations who prefer larger congregations and a livelier scene.

The second reason that most churches do not grow is that many congregants are steeped in their own traditions, and are unfamiliar with seismic changes that have occurred in American religion. Church leaders, along with rank and file members, are largely unaware that many attractive alternatives in worship, service, and community are readily available to them.

The third reason is that church members tend to be content with the familiar, and resist changes that would rearrange the standing order. The status quo in congregational life is exceptionally deep-seated. Church members may see few reasons to change much that is currently in place. Longer-term members also presume that new members, including younger generations, will adopt the policies and practices that older generations put in place, perhaps decades ago.

In many churches, new members are not expected to bring forth new ideas until they understand, "How we do things around here." UUs tend to view themselves as liberal and open-minded. But ministers of numerous faiths claim that theologically liberal congregations are more resistant to new ideas than conservative congregations.

In my experience as a parish consultant, I find that UU congregations possess a limited capacity for systemic change. This occurs, in large part, because of a diverse theology and various factions that exist within the membership. For example, proposed changes in worship or music run a high risk of being opposed by various combinations of theists, deists, humanists, atheists, agnostics, pagans, people of different generations, and the ubiquitous vocal minority that seems to exist in all UU congregations.

Attempts to make changes in congregational life reveal that the more diverse the theology, the greater the likelihood of internal dissent.

Diversity is the ultimate UU dogma, but the emphasis on "all voices being heard" creates congregations whose dominant attributes are maintaining harmony and keeping various factions content. Fear of controversy can paralyze a congregation, ensuring that it maintains existing habits and ways.

I am familiar with numerous UU congregations whose clergy and board members literally live in fear of displeasing various segments of the congregation. But maintaining harmony, according to Congregational minister Anthony Robinson, "Is often an inability to deal with the tough questions or to be honest with one another."[2]

UU congregations offer people of all beliefs a place at the table. This is a unique strength. However, being seated at the table cannot be the culmination of congregational life. The culture of, "We are here and we are diverse" is not enough. The culture of, "I have my beliefs and you have yours, end of discussion" is also insufficient. Diversity must serve as a platform by which people of dissimilar beliefs unite in common cause for a greater purpose.

To a congregation's detriment, attempts to keep various groups satisfied result in a "lowest common denominator" religion, one that tries to be all things to all people. This is the primary reason why many UU congregations and the larger movement reflect little coherence. Church programs proliferate to accommodate scores of interests, but there is little sense of a bigger picture or recognizable direction.

Columnist George Will addressed this particular issue when he led an informal discussion about the Episcopal Church, of which he is a lifelong member. He said, "The church's leadership has become latitudinarian – tolerant to the point of incoherence. The Episcopal Church used to be a bridge between Catholicism and Protestantism. Now it is a bridge between Protestantism and the secular, anything goes, culture."

An emphasis on diversity and something for everyone prevents UU congregations from uniting behind vital, timely, soul-stirring initiatives. (In my work with congregations from coast to coast, I find that UUs steadfastly refuse to believe that diversity can be a weakness, despite the credibility of the source.)

Sunday school aside, most UU congregations are oriented toward meeting the desires of the aforementioned factions and current members who are 50 years of age or older. No plans exist to turn the church over to younger generations who will chart a future course. This is not the congregation of tomorrow.

## The nature and character of Unitarian Universalism itself

Many tenets on which Unitarian Universalism rests also relegate the movement to a former era. Unitarian Universalism is characterized by:

- Diversity of belief
- Low expectations of membership and charitable giving
- A reliance on reason and intellect
- Personal autonomy
- Traditional forms of worship
- Attempts to be all things to all people
- An abhorrence of evangelism
- Distrust of clergy leadership
- An emphasis on the democratic process
- A hands-off attitude toward encouraging members to lead lives of dedication, commitment, and when necessary, sacrifice for the greater good

As a UU of 30 years standing, it pains me to say that almost nothing on this list appeals to church-shopping Americans today. Those seeking a church do so because they are lost or lonely, are hurting in body or soul, are searching for lives of greater meaning and purpose, are concerned about their finances or their careers, wish to raise happy and healthy children, yearn to understand a world that is increasingly uncertain, wish to forgive or be forgiven, and desire to create a more equitable society.

Church shoppers have little interest in personal autonomy, individual freedom, or the democratic process. They are seeking a church that will challenge their self-centeredness, one that offers an alternative to a consumer oriented society and its attendant shallowness. And, they are willing to invest considerable time, energy, and money to achieve these goals. They are yearning to be asked to make a commitment.

This returns us to redefining the UU "product." Challenging any of the established tenets listed above is not only difficult, but in my experience with some congregations, foolhardy. Some congregations wear metaphorical suits of armor in regard to anything other than that tweaking the current scheme of things.

At the denominational level, a focus on social issues, many carried forward from the 1960s, has inhibited bringing up new generations of church "planters," clergy and lay leaders who know how to start new churches. The denomination has also not created a cadre of church "transformers," people who are skilled in helping established congregations keep pace with changing times.

## The contemporary church: a new species in American religion

Growth in membership is not the only criterion to measure a congregation's effectiveness. But we need to consider why some churches grow and others do not. Churches that are growing (both liberal and conservative) have well-defined agendas and clearly articulated purposes, i.e., this is who we are and what we teach. They set forth core values that unite people in shared community. These churches project higher expectations of membership and charitable giving. Many of these churches routinely include changes in worship that come as surprises on Sunday morning.[3] If potential new members do not wish to meet the standards set forth, they are not allowed to join the church.

Growing congregations often proclaim, "This is the journey we are on. Come join us!" They do not convene focus groups or hold congregational votes to determine what the journey will be. Unlike churches of an earlier era, growing, activist congregations tend not to assert their agendas into local or national politics. These churches support AIDS research, confront child poverty in their communities, are concerned about environmental issues, and focus on human need. Whether church members are politically liberal or conservative is irrelevant.

When people join such a progressive church, they are expected to change the way they conduct their daily lives, to live faithfully in community with fellow congregants. Changes may include foregoing alcohol and tobacco, setting one day each week apart for rest and reflection, giving 5 to 10 percent of one's income to the church or other causes, developing a spiritual discipline, and a commitment to working outside the church for the common good.

Progressive churches frequently undertake new ministries and outreach efforts even when adequate funds are not available. I recall one minister saying, "We're going to need another $35,000 this year and I have no idea where the money will come from. But in my 23 years of ministry, it has always shown up!"

Progressive churches strive for restlessness rather than familiarity, reach out to wandering souls, and express an eagerness to experiment with new forms of community and service. Their orientation is toward the future, toward people not yet encountered. This combination of factors has created congregations that reach across the generations. Exact numbers are hard to come by, but an estimated 20,000 new congregations that function on this model have been founded in the past 25 years.

UUs often discount the church just described, claiming that members are unthinking automatons. I'm not suggesting these churches are the epitome of congregational life. They have their shortcomings, and are not everyone's cup of tea. But UUs should not readily dismiss this influential aspect of contemporary American religion. Progressive churches have evolved to meet the challenges of a changing world, and have tapped into powerful religious sentiments of the American public.

For example, a large billboard in Southern California proclaims, "Mission Gathering Christian Church is sorry for the narrow-minded, judgmental, deceptive actions of those who took away the rights and equalities of so many in the name of God. Our hearts are with you. Christianity for all!" This is a perfect example of how contemporary churches have created an entire new language and sense of being.

Churches like these, frequently nondenominational, are a new species on the American religious landscape. They began to spring up in the 1970s and 80s because the founding ministers of these congregations believed the traditional church could not be reformed. They realized that millions of people were seeking an alternative to the church of their parents and grandparents.

## Closer to home: reasons why UU congregations have not grown

It's also instructive to view our religious movement at the congregational level. Some churches in the 10 percent that are growing have conducted capital campaigns for new construction or building renovations, and foresee a new tomorrow. They are to be commended. I have visited many of these churches, and have been heartened by the congregation's excitement about its role in the larger community.

In the remaining 90 percent of UU congregations, and sometimes even in the top 10 percent, perennial budget constraints often prevent evocative visions from being formulated. Having little money to consider anything new, even in affluent congregations, creates a tendency to maintain accustomed ways. Church newsletters from five, ten, or twenty years ago may be remarkably similar to those of last week.

UU congregations have also not grown, nor created compelling visions, because they exhibit little sense of urgency. Churches of many faiths and many sizes often behave as though nothing important is at stake.[4]

With no soul-stirring vision, little sense of urgency, and continual budget constraints, the typical church in America remains remarkably similar year-to-year. Visitors often perceive the social needs of current members being met, but do not find the spiritual depth they seek. The church appears to be a type of guild for those who already belong. Visitors often feel they have intruded upon a family reunion.

First-time visitors often report that attending the Sunday service is a disheartening experience. Visitors frequently sit by themselves in the pews. They stand alone in coffee hour holding red visitor's mugs or wearing guest nametags, only to be ignored by the rest of the congregation. Single and divorced adults tell me they feel lonelier when visiting a church than at any other time. Churches convey subtle but powerful messages that a visitor "is not one of us." Few religious leaders understand what it's like for an outsider to break into the "holy huddle."[5]

We should keep in mind the perspective of Chris Sonkin, president of the consulting firm, Real Church Solutions. Among the services he provides are mystery worshipers, people who attend various churches to rate congregations on a list of criteria. Mystery worshipers are a growing phenomenon in the church world, as clergy and lay leaders desire an accurate portrait of congregational life that can be found no other way. Sonkin notes, "First-time guests don't come with mercy, they come with judgment. They are looking for a reason to leave."[6]

Beyond the experience of being a visitor is the worship service itself. I have attended and participated in memorable UU worship services that touched my heart, soul, and mind. I stand in awe of UU ministers whose guiding words have changed my life for the better. I believe that liberal religion's powerful message rivals any faith or theology.

But the norm in many UU churches on Sunday morning is otherwise. The service often begins with announcements, sometimes lengthy and read haltingly by someone who is excessively nervous and puts the congregation on edge. A hymn might follow, but UUs, similar to Catholics playfully described by Garrison Keillor on his *Prairie Home Companion* radio show, tend to be diffident singers, so this is a lackluster experience. Next might come a reading whose intellectual content is difficult for listeners to discern. A children's story may follow, customarily secular in nature, about planting a garden or making a quilt, no different from what a child encounters at school or the library. Sometimes a parishioner or two, dressed in madcap attire, act out a skit that announces an upcoming event. Since most churches do not have the resources for professional musicians, the volunteer choir strives mightily but its singing is frequently uninspired. People coming forward to share joys and concerns (that some find meaningful and others find irksome) can be an uncertain proposition, as parishioners now and again ramble on about their children's accomplishments or travel adventures. An exceptional sermon from the minister or a visiting speaker will moderate this environment favorably, but that's not a given.

Some view these worship elements as "chatty" rather than religious. Those who grew up in formal religious traditions perceive humorous announcements as out of place in worship, bordering on the sacrilegious. Many Sunday services are also conducted at a painstakingly slow pace. These factors create congregations whose worship life is humdrum, based on an Order of Service that dates back 150 years that is kept intact by force of habit rather than an adaptation to a changing world.

At the social hour, off-brand coffee and powdered cream provide yet another stark contrast between a 1950s church and the contemporary Starbucks world. Nationwide, less than half of UUs and liberal Protestants attend Sunday worship, for these very reasons. When half or more of the membership doesn't bother to show up, isn't this an unmistakable signal of the need for profound change?

I admit that I find meaning in certain elements of traditional worship. But an emphasis on old forms will relegate a congregation to days gone by. Visitors from younger generations often perceive the Sunday service described above as amateur in nature. They expect a high quality experience because they were raised in a world that provides superior media, sight, and sound. It's the thirty-three and a third LP generation attempting to reach the iPod generation.

Speaking of generational differences, more than 27,000 churches have created profiles on www.mychurch.org, since 2006. This site, similar to Facebook and My Space, offer worship and social networking opportunities for young adults. Using the Internet and language that is familiar to younger generations help churches appear current and up-to-date. Included in the opportunities are off-site worship services and various other church-related gatherings, complete with Google maps.

Some gatherings are held at bars, restaurants, and brewpubs, because that's where young people are having discussions about things that matter. At many of these gatherings, attendees become involved in the big questions of life, such as faith, war, relationships, sexuality, and what's wrong with religion that it has not yet spoken to them. These churches function on the basis of going where people are, rather than waiting for them to show up at the front door.

Hundreds of contemporary churches also utilize password-protected blogs, to encourage questions and discussion among members and church seekers alike.[7] This is a church world almost completely unknown to older generations.

Older church members desire to preserve what has worked for them, and their children and grandchildren are their hope for making this happen. However, in many families those children and grandchildren have dropped out of church altogether or moved to a more generationally friendly church and worship style. They do not wish to perpetuate the old, but create the new.[8]

Ministers, religious educators, and lay leaders need to realize that attitudes among young Americans have truly changed. The culture has moved light years past the skeptical attitudes that churchgoers faced in earlier generations; when young people rebelled and then, as they grew older, returned to traditional forms of faith.

In Lyle Schaller's enlightening book, *44 Ways to Increase Church Attendance*, the first recommendation is to augment the quality of the Sunday service. This can be accomplished by offering a message of hope, enhancing the quality of preaching by expanding the number of speakers, by changing the music, and by quickening the pace. The remaining 40 ways offer fascinating reading for those who desire to see new faces on Sunday morning.[9]

## One additional reason why growth has not occurred

Members of UU and liberal Protestant congregations are customarily reluctant to talk with others about their faith. Doing so would be considered that dreaded evangelism, an activity consigned to right wing faiths and beneath our dignity. I lived in New England long enough to learn that religion is kept private. We would never push our views onto others, and UU evangelists are rare.

But word of mouth is the most effective way to grow congregations, as about 70 percent of people in all churches are there because someone invited them. However, this simple, inexpensive, and effective method for growing UU congregations is rarely discussed, let alone encouraged.

Thus, most congregations expect new people to find the church on their own, usually from seeing an ad in the newspaper or visiting an Internet website. Current members need only wait for them to arrive. I've actually heard board presidents say there is no need to "recruit" new members. If you peruse guest books in the vestibules of most UU churches, you'll find that visitors are few and far between. This is unmistakable evidence that a laissez-faire attitude of attracting new members works poorly.

Since merger in 1961, Unitarian Universalism has remained on a plateau in membership during a time in which the population of the United States has almost doubled. "Growth" in the movement has been about one new member per church per year. Reasonable minds might conclude that strategies for growing in membership have not been successful. Ad campaigns sponsored by the denomination will be ineffective when the product being marketed has little appeal to contemporary church seekers.

If you're looking for some good news, Schaller's formula for growth that follows will offset the entrenched attitudes just enumerated that do not serve us well.

## Lyle Schaller's membership concept

The question at hand is who new members will be. As mentioned, most churches believe it will be whoever happens to show up. We hope to attract everyone, and not exclude anyone.

Congregations of all denominations need to identify a future constituency. Who new members be? A future constituency cannot be left to chance. But it is infinitely logical to appeal to all potential comers. However, the "y'all come" mentality has resulted in no growth for almost 50 years, and is a guaranteed way to ensure that 90 percent of UU congregations will remain on plateaus or decline in membership in the years to come.

Congregations of many faiths also tend to believe their future lies exclusively with young families. Or, that a young, attractive, energetic minister with small children will arrive on the scene and turn things around. These churches could not be more mistaken. Many congregations cannot compete with neighboring churches that have newer facilities and family-friendly programs. In addition, current members may be unwilling to make the trade-offs required to serve such a population. Price tags often include new or renovated classrooms, bathrooms, and kitchens; and perhaps a change in the Sunday morning worship schedule.

To identify a future constituency and grow in membership, Schaller recommends that churches reach out to specific groups, or cohorts of the population.[10] Examples include:

Single-parent families
Mature adults, over 50 years of age
Recently divorced or widowed adults
People whose families include an alcoholic member
Families that include someone who is battling cancer
Families with teenagers
Single people between the ages of 25 and 35
People or families that have experienced tragedy
Former Christians who have become un-churched
Gay and lesbian singles or couples
People in interfaith marriages or families
People who live within walking distance to the church
Families that include members with physical disabilities
Interracial couples or families
Military families

You may certainly add other segments of the population to this list, depending on the community in which your church is located.

To attract any segment of the population requires clergy, lay leaders, or people in the pews who currently represent that particular cohort; who are willing to reach out and engage others in their group.

The ground rules do not permit you to review the list of cohorts and say, "We should be able to attract all these people." Only churches of 2,500 members or more have the staff, resources, and facilities to engage a widely diverse population.

Reaching out to potential members instead of waiting for people to show up is a significant departure from the membership norm. In order to grow, church members need to become proactive in bringing others into community. Many churches claim they wish to grow, but do little other than voice this sentiment.

*Church growth is not dependent solely on the minister, the staff, or the board. Rather, growth is a responsibility of rank and file members to reach out to others in need.*

The question that logically follows is, "Why would any cohort be attracted to this congregation?" What do we offer that would be of interest?" This may be a difficult question to answer. The ground rules also do not permit you to say, "We have an open-minded faith, and that should be enough for all groups."

## Who are potential UUs?

For most churchgoers, it is reassuring to discover that new members are PLU, people like us. It's heartening to see that new members are educated, successful, have well-behaved children, and can take care of themselves. Congregational life will go on as before. New members who fit this description are low maintenance, and we hope they will give more than they ask in return. Most churches prefer new members to be the saved and the found, not those who tossed to and fro by life's travails.

But what if a congregation engages a sizable group of adults who are recently widowed or divorced? Or, if the church engages a dozen families that include an alcoholic member? Or families that have experienced tragedy? These are not the saved and the found, low maintenance types we prefer. They may require more than they can give in return. They may not be people with whom we would ordinarily associate. Will they be welcome? Do they fall under the UU definition of diversity?

Adding a dozen families from a particular cohort may also mean that a sizable number of new faces materialize suddenly. Congregations of 150 members can assimilate eight or ten new members each year, but what if 12 new families of moms, dads, kids, and cousins total 50 people altogether? This would expand the congregation's size by a third. How will the congregation accommodate a large influx of people they don't know?

It is tempting to think a congregation can grow numerically without changing anything that is currently in place. Church members expect new people to blend into the existing system. But attracting new cohorts of the population will require trade-offs. For example,

- *If the church attracted military families, would current members be comfortable seeing people on Sunday morning in uniform? Would current members feel comfortable with families who may support military action in foreign lands?*

- *Churches wishing to attract younger generations would require contemporary (rock-oriented) music at worship, or an additional worship service with contemporary music. Going this route would have both cultural and budgetary implications. Would the leadership and current members support this?*
- *If churches wish to attract those who are currently un-churched, this would mean a significant increase in members talking about the church with others, and 10 percent of the budget spent on marketing. Would current members consider this scenario if it was presented to them?*
- *If churches wish to reach out to minority groups, this might mean a new worship service in a different language, or incorporating a second language into the existing worship service. Would such changes acceptable to current members?*

The above scenarios might be exciting to some, while others may believe the trade-offs are too high. But one fact is certain. UU congregations believing they can attract anyone and everyone will remain on plateaus or decline in membership. Fifty years of evidence make this an irrefutable fact.

## Evangelism reconsidered

While this chapter is about church growth, a paradox is that reaching out to various cohorts of the population should not be viewed strictly as a growth strategy. Growth in membership may be the eventual result, but the emphasis should be on the congregation's eagerness to reach out to the larger world.

This perspective makes evangelism considerably more palatable. For example, most UUs would rarely, if ever, invite their friends, neighbors, or co-workers to church. However, it is perfectly acceptable for congregants to say, "Our church hosts a dinner for single-parent families (or any other cohort) on the first Saturday of each month. The purpose is not to evangelize, but to provide companionship and support to families in need. If you know any single parents, I hope you will mention this gathering to them."

Our Universalist heritage reminds us of the great human family of which we are a part. Expanding this family is one of our highest and noblest callings. This is the true definition of diversity, the public church that we should create, one that reaches out to those in need.

An added benefit is that engaging previously unknown people and helping them along life's journey is the surest path to finding truth, spirituality, peace, and enlightenment for ourselves.

CHAPTER 3

# Leadership Makes it or Breaks It

*People are only as creative as the congregational structure allows them to be.*
— Rick Warren, minister of Saddleback Community Church and author of *The Purpose Driven Life*

A few years ago I was working with the Board of Trustees at a sizeable UU congregation. We were discussing the importance of leadership. About 10 minutes into the conversation a board member said, "I'm unsure about my colleagues, but I don't perceive myself as a leader of this congregation." A pause ensued. Board members looked at one another in a tentative manner.

I asked the remaining eight board members if they viewed themselves as leaders. Only three did. A troubled look came over the minister's face. After awhile, a board member who had not spoken previously said, "I believe we act as caretakers rather than leaders." This was an unsettling insight for them.

A few months later I asked the same question of another Board of Trustees at a different church. I wondered if I would find a similar result. This time, I asked board members to place themselves along the spectrum of leader to caretaker. Five people on this 11-member board perceived themselves as leaders. One person added an extremely enlightened perspective. She said, "I don't believe leadership is expected of us."

In my work with numerous congregations since, the highest proportion of board members who consider themselves leaders is 55 percent. More troubling, however, is that most board members do not believe that leadership is actually desired of them.

I hasten to add that being a leader or a caretaker are equally valuable roles, and are sometimes interchangeable. Churches require many caretakers. These are usually dependable souls who handle myriad details that make congregations effective in what they do. Sometimes caretakers assume leadership roles, and sometimes leaders complete a term on the board or a committee, then step back and allow others to take up leadership positions. This back-and-forth helps create healthy congregations, with people assuming multiple tasks.

One exception to revolving roles is that board members who served in the 1970s, 80s, and 90s should not return to the board for additional terms. While well intentioned, former leaders tend to visualize the church of yesterday, not the church of tomorrow.

While on this subject, when a board president's term expires, he or she should not remain on the board as past president. The reason is that some initiatives put forth by past presidents may have outlived their usefulness. If a former president remains on the board, such initiatives will be exceedingly difficult to discontinue if that person is still in the room.

As important as leaders and caretakers are, these roles are distinctly different. Leaders envision the future. Caretakers manage day-to-day functions. Too often, though, leaders behave as functionaries. This creates an emphasis on the everyday and the current fiscal year rather than longer-term initiatives and adapting to an ever-changing world. By the way, the concept of leaders and caretakers applies to boards that utilize the policy governance approach, as well as those that employ the traditional board model.

*Leaders create a congregation in their own image, for better or worse. A strong board will challenge and empower a congregation to consider new ways to expand its ministry. A hesitant, cautious board will create a congregation that has little courage or fervor to chart a new course.*

## A closer look at the role of leadership

At any given moment, a member of a nominating committee may be calling a fellow congregant with an invitation to join the board. Too many of these invitations consist of remarks such as, "You don't have to do a whole lot. The board meets monthly except for July and August, and it mostly keeps track of the budget and reviews committee reports." Large churches often hold elections and candidates put themselves forward, but most churches select board members via the nomination process.

Asking potential board members for a token effort is a surefire formula for ineffective leadership. Anyone who accepts such an invitation should not serve in a leadership role. An ambiguous invitation also conveys the impression that the board merely perpetuates what is currently in place.

Few churches have written job descriptions for board members. Little thought seems to go into the content of the job, as well. Can you imagine taking a paid job that had no description of your duties and responsibilities? (A job description follows later in this chapter.)

Most people who are asked to serve on the board are successful professionally, or are capable in some aspect of their personal lives. That's why they were selected. Once on the board, however, chances are they will be marginally effective in their new positions. The primary reason, in addition to an ambiguous role, is that congregations provide insufficient orientation or training.

An apt analogy is UUs being invited to serve on the boards of a local hospital, theater group, arts organization, dance company, public library, or agency that serves people with mental illness. Would any of these UUs, potential board members, know enough about these organizations to make informed decisions? Not likely. Yet early in their tenures, new church board members often make decisions that involve hundreds of thousands of dollars, knowing little about the nature of the religious communities they serve.

Sometimes churches hold board retreats, in which new members are provided an update on initiatives in progress and what the coming year might bring. These gatherings can be very helpful. But in my experience, such meetings are based on local tradition and tend to perpetuate existing customs and habits. New board members are expected to act as replacements for those who rotate off, and function in ways similar to their predecessors.

Leadership theories abound, and my intention is not to promote one theory or another. Rather, I believe board members, whether old or new, work from a marked disadvantage. That disadvantage is unfamiliarity with church literature. Most lay leaders have not been introduced to an extraordinarily interesting body of congregational writings. They do not realize this literature is readily accessible to them, or how a little homework would make them considerably more effective in their roles. The elementary point I wish to make is that informed leaders are more capable than uninformed leaders.

For example, Lyle Schaller's books are among the best ever written. For board members of small congregations, under 100 at Sunday worship, I recommend *The Small Membership Church*. For leaders of somewhat larger congregations, 100 to 250 at Sunday worship, I recommend *The Middle Sized Church*. For leaders of larger congregations, those with 250 or more at Sunday services, I recommend *The Seven Day A Week Church*.[1]

Schaller writes from a Christian perspective, but his advice is applicable to all congregations. Don't be concerned that his books were written some time ago. They are timeless. Three other books of his that are extremely good are *Activating the Passive Church, 44 Steps Up Off the Plateau,* and, *44 Ways to Expand the Financial Base of Your Congregation*.[2]

Without access to church literature, board members bring their secular experience to the institution of the church. Churches are the ultimate volunteer organizations, and function very differently from the paid workplace. Board members require insight into congregational life that church literature provides. Church boards cannot function on an amateur, uninformed basis.

As a congregation grows in size and complexity, strong, well-informed clergy and lay leadership becomes essential. By strong leaders, I do not mean authoritarian leaders. Informed leadership is an indispensable key to any congregation's future. For those who are wary of strong clergy or lay leadership, I question what the advantage of weak leadership would be. Would any of us desire ineffective leadership of our town's schools, hospitals, or local government?

Informed and respected leadership does not happen by chance. It needs to be earned. Congregations are seldom healthier than their leaders, and if a congregation's leaders believe their lives are enhanced and their spirits deepened, they will set an example for rank and file members.

All congregations need to maintain a high caliber of leadership. Some boards "click" and some don't. Some boards function successfully but then a few key players rotate off and the magic is lost. Probability is not good enough. Thus, I recommend a *Covenant of Leadership*, a type of job description, which will ensure more consistent, effective leadership. This covenant should include:

- *The church being a leader's primary volunteer commitment beyond normal family obligations.*
- *Believing that leaders are leading the congregation somewhere, not just overseeing finance, administration, and care of the property.*

- *Reading articles and books by prominent church writers, to understand more fully the nature and character of faith communities.*
- *Visiting churches of other faiths, including those more conservative, to gain a broader perspective of contemporary American religion.*
- *Working with the minister to develop a spiritual discipline, otherwise leadership will resemble that of a secular organization.*
- *Reaching the 5 to 10 percent charitable giving level as soon as possible.*
- *Embodying the belief that the congregation should function from an attitude of abundance and not scarcity.*
- *Recognizing one important law of congregations, which is, "Churches that reach out will thrive. Those that focus on their own members will eventually decline."*
- *Helping the congregation adapt to a rapidly changing world by encouraging younger members to bring new ideas and assume leadership roles.*
- *Being willing to take risks to enhance congregational life.*
- *Recognizing that a leader's role is not to please everyone.*
- *Saying "yes" to as many new ideas as possible.*

The higher the standards placed on a congregation's leadership, the more healthy a congregation will be. Confident leaders create confident congregations because the commitment, spiritual growth, and charitable giving of members will rise to that of the leadership. Leaders need to be reminded continually that their roles involve modeling a way of life for people in the pews.

Potential board members should be given a copy of this covenant (or some variation thereof, but not too watered down) to review before they accept an invitation to serve. Churches require people of good character and commitment, and raising the bar will not chase qualified people away but will attract those who take their roles seriously. If board members strive to meet the requirements of the Covenant of Leadership, this will bind them together in common purpose.

Actually, many of the elements in the above covenant might apply to all church members and friends, as well. Don't you think?

The future of any congregation depends on informed leaders who have done their homework, surveyed the local scene, and can point the congregation to a promising tomorrow. As previously mentioned, the congregation's message should be, "This is the journey upon which we are embarked. Come join us." If the leadership sets a steady course, congregants of good will are likely to honor that leadership with their moral and financial support.

## Clergy Leadership

Thus far, we've focused on lay leadership. Now we turn to clergy, either the senior minister in a multi-staff environment, sole pastor, or an associate minister. The minister's role, regardless of where he or she is located on the organizational chart, is crucial to any congregation that wishes to venture beyond its current status.

Paul Nixon is author of the book, *I Refuse to Lead a Dying Congregation*. He is a former Southern Baptist who eventually became a progressive Methodist minister. His unorthodox religious journey has provided him keen insight into the role of clergy as effective leaders. He identifies a number of characteristics of ministers who lead successful congregations:

- *The passionate conviction that churches offer something that will renew human lives and communities.*
- *The determination to clear some new territory – to push the church to new places and new people.*
- *The belief that a congregation in this particular place and time exists to do something important.*
- *A clear and surprisingly simple sense of mission.*
- *Attraction toward friends and relationships on the edge of conventional church circles and often far beyond.*
- *An awareness of the ways that organized religion has stopped short of living out its good news.*
- *Boredom with unchanging routines and maintenance tasks.*
- *The capacity to communicate the church's spiritual experience and vision winsomely to others, so they are persuaded to jump aboard the bandwagon.*[3]

Nixon then notes, "These characteristics make no reference to left, right, or middle theological positions. And yet, liberal Protestant denominations have relatively few clergy who would be described as possessing these characteristics. We on the left are usually oriented toward different emphases and goals than growing churches and leading people to faith."

Nixon continues his observation by adding," The liberal church's different emphases may include educating others about the need for a Palestinian homeland; climate change; or at a local level, helping create affordable housing. These are holy tasks. But if we are not about creating more adherents who will serve humanity in these ways, our efforts in the years to come will dry up because we will dry up."[4]

## A new challenge and a real-life example

As noted, church boards tend to focus on administration, finance, and care of the property. These issues constrain a congregation's leadership because they steer board members into a maintenance posture. Sometimes, board meetings begin with the treasurer projecting a financial shortfall. This fosters an attitude of paucity toward remaining items on the agenda.

A culture of scarcity creates leaders who believe their primary role is to limit expenses rather than expand the ministry of the congregation. The result is an attitude of caution interjected into board deliberations, which in turn creates docility in a congregation. Sadly, the minutes of board meetings that are printed in church newsletters are often the most uninspiring part of the entire publication.

The issue at hand is not methods of governance, such as the traditional board structure vs. policy governance. Rather, 21st century congregations require a completely different type of leadership.

> *The challenge [of the contemporary church] is how to shift its ministry from the top-down, minister-centered model of the 1950s to a bottom up, organic, collegial, permission-granting, team-oriented model centered around the spiritual giftedness of its members.*[5]

Let me provide a first-hand example of how this forward-looking concept is frequently thwarted. I recently attended a board meeting of an extremely wealthy congregation. A respected layperson requested time on the agenda to speak of her dream, a new service on Sunday afternoon that would feature Gregorian chant.

She had seen similar services at two other churches and believed a Sunday afternoon gathering would reach a new segment of the population and enhance congregational life in general. The board agreed. She was willing to plan and coordinate this new service. She estimated the cost to be about $9,000 for the first year. Board members listened politely as she described how she would manage all the arrangements; including her intention of submitting a grant proposal to a foundation in New York, over 2,500 miles away. This foundation had no prior knowledge of the church.

When she finished her presentation, board members thanked her and she left the room. The board took up the next item on the agenda. It was clear to all present that her chances of getting a grant were nonexistent. The Sunday service she proposed would have no chance of being enacted. The quote from Rick Warren at the beginning of this chapter played out as he observed – people are only as creative as the structure allows them to be. This church's Board of Trustees was a barrier to innovation and creativity.

The board's passivity toward a respected layperson with a provocative idea embodies the top-down, permission-denying approach that is characteristic of church governing bodies. Board members offered no encouragement and no assistance to a competent person from its own ranks. No board member suggested that seed money might be found in the budget, or that the congregation be asked to fund this new aspect of church life, or that a small amount be taken from the church's sizeable unrestricted endowment to prime the pump. She was on her own.

Board members did not empower the spiritual giftedness this woman embodied, or her leadership capability. Without realizing it, board members had done this woman and the congregation a great disservice. I suspect the woman in question is unlikely to present another new idea.

Some might claim this congregant didn't know how to work the system. Others might recall organizational literature that suggests the best way to kill a good idea is to refer it to a committee.

The church's finances also played a large role in determining the fate of the proposed Sunday service. This affluent church displayed a high level of financial anxiety and functioned from a, "tyranny of the operating budget" mentality. If it's not in the budget, we can't do it. This church asked members for financial support only once each year during the annual pledge drive, and pledges had been flat for several years. Thus, new initiatives were rare, even in a congregation in which money was no object.

## An alternative approach

In contrast, the bottom-up, collegial, team-oriented, permission-granting approach might have yielded a different result. In churches that have adopted a permission-granting policy, a person who has a new idea that falls within the vision and purpose of the congregation is automatically granted permission to proceed.

Since the idea of a service with Gregorian chant did fall within the church's vision, this woman could have proceeded with confidence. However, one ground rule is that church members cannot undertake new initiatives on their own. They must have at least two other members as working partners. This alleviates the fear of "loose cannons" who act solely in the name of the church.

If the church just mentioned had a team-oriented approach toward its work and future, the minister would have given this woman the green light and she would have found kindred spirits on that team who could offer guidance and support. Board approval is not required. Additional church members could have been enlisted in this new aspect of church life. Some may have contributed financially. All would have become empowered to create a new form of ministry.

The church of tomorrow is one that wholeheartedly embraces entrepreneurial ministry. It is one that encourages imaginative souls who wish to create new forms of congregational life and service. In my experience, congregations that accomplish this believe that new ideas beget new ideas, and that enthusiasm begets even greater enthusiasm.

For example, I have worked with congregations that embodied a core value of giving away up to 30 percent of their budgets to outreach beyond their own four walls. The leadership in these churches believes that spreading money around inspired new forms of ministry and empowerment. Church leaders are confident that the money will always be there, and congregants believe they can do anything they set their mind to.

The most spectacular example of the accomplishment conviction is Memorial Drive Presbyterian Church in Houston, Texas. This church gives away one dollar to the needs of the world for every dollar it spends on itself. This 3,000-member church gives away millions of dollars. The members of this church are little different in socioeconomic status than most UU congregations. Achieving this monumental feat is within the range of UU churches, fellowships, and societies.

Conversely, I recently worked with an affluent church that has a $1.7 million endowment and no debt. The congregation recently voted not to increase the 1.5 percent line item for outreach because of an attitude of acute scarcity. The congregation held a vote because board members were fearful of making a decision and didn't want to offend anyone. In the end, the vote was 52 to 48 percent against, consigning the congregation to a minimalist role in the community and disillusioning half its members. This is a textbook example of how weak leadership failed in its rightful duty and created a congregation in its own image. The members of this church were the most parsimonious, passive, and least involved in ministry of any congregation I've ever known.

In all instances cited in this chapter, the leadership influenced the behavior of the congregation. The method of governance did not determine the significant differences between decisions that were made. Rather, the adventurous congregations had chosen spiritually mature leaders who lived out their religious values, served as role models for their congregants, and instilled a sense of confidence in the congregation as a whole. These leaders believed that something important was at stake.

How did they accomplish this? These church leaders did not focus on administration and finance. They created congregations whose members were challenged to go deeper into the faith. These church leaders were not satisfied with things as they were.

Rev. Anthony Robinson writes of this attitude in a compelling way. "Never to challenge, question, disorient, or lead people onto risky terrain," he claims, "can hardly be called leadership. It may be a fine institutional chaplaincy, but it is not pastoral leadership. When things are too placid, leaders should stir things up, start some trouble."[6]

UUs claim a history of radical ideas. Now is the time to reclaim that heritage and empower our congregations to dream, and accomplish, new and wondrous dreams.

CHAPTER 4

# Creating Committed Members: New Ideas. Lasting Results

*We strive to create committed members. Creating uncommitted members doesn't do them or the church any good.*
— Presbyterian minister Jane Worthington

If UU congregations could do one thing that would make them healthier and stronger-minded, it would be to raise the expectations, importance, and meaning of membership.

Low expectations of membership rank extremely high in Unitarian Universalism's shortcomings. Many church leaders are hesitant to ask current or potential members to do much, or to give much in terms of financial support. This attitude stems from a deep-seated though erroneous belief that asking people to make a commitment will drive them away. In the United States today, the fastest growing churches, liberal and conservative, project higher expectations of membership.

> *Creating higher-expectation congregations is an essential key to Unitarian Universalism's future. Members and friends should desire a church that asks something meaningful of them.*

Actually, higher expectation membership already exists. Every congregation contains a segment of stalwart members who set high expectations for themselves. These steadfast souls are dedicated, committed, and stand ever ready to pitch in, whatever the need. UU churches should strive to turn out people just like this. It is perfectly acceptable to ask all church members to be dedicated members.

I recall a minister telling her teenage children, "When you are adults, I expect you to be UUs, to be generous donors, and to take leadership roles in your chosen congregations. This is what religion is all about. Church will be an important part of your lives."

About a week later I read the newsletter column of another UU minister who wrote, "We certainly can't expect our children to remain UUs when they are adults. The best we can do is give them the freedom to choose a faith, or not choose a faith if they so desire." Each is a self-fulfilling prophecy. Which point of view will ensure the future of Unitarian Universalism? Which point of view does your congregation convey to children and youth?

People yearn to be a meaningful part of meaningful organizations, including congregations. By making membership discretionary or effortless, we devalue its importance and its power to influence people's lives for the better.

Devaluation of membership is a primary factor in creating systemic weakness in UU congregations across the land. In most churches, approximately 25 percent of the membership does the lion's share of the work and gives most of the money. The remaining three-quarters get an economical (sometimes free) ride because low expectations of membership have given them permission to do so.

I recall a *liberal* Methodist minister saying, "This church is not a sailing vessel with a small number of people down in the hold, rowing with the oars, while a larger number of passengers occupy the first class deck, enjoying the view, especially those who didn't buy a ticket to get on board!" This church promoted equal opportunity to serve. Potential members were told if they didn't envision participating at an elevated level, they should look elsewhere for a church. The congregation's logo on its newsletter is, "The Adventure of a Lifetime Begins Here." This congregation behaves accordingly, and is one of the most adventurous, lively congregations I've ever encountered.

## What membership should mean

UU congregations would do well to consider the concept of, "Integrity of membership," or, "Membership with authenticity." Membership in UU congregations should include:

- Attending Sunday services regularly
- Participating in one program each year that deepens your faith
- Participating in one outreach or mission project each year

- Reaching the 5 to 10 percent giving level as soon as possible
- Telling others about the church

Some readers may view these criteria for membership as reasonable, a low rung on the ladder. Others might view them as wildly unrealistic, that UU churches could never ask people for so much. Members who joined the church with low expectations and have become accustomed to a low commitment environment may be startled that more would be expected of them. But those who desire a comfortable church are not the ones who should determine the expectations of membership.

Be forewarned that some members may state emphatically, "No one in this church will attend services regularly, or give that much money." What they are saying is that they, themselves, will not meet these standards. They are also attempting to project their beliefs onto the congregation as a whole. This should not be permitted. Other members, in fact, may feel quite differently.

When people join a church, they are the most open to new ideas than at any other time. Gordon Atkinson, a Baptist minister known as the Real Live Preacher, is more theologically liberal than most UUs. He is correct when he writes, "People long for a spiritual journey and not a religious assimilation."[1] When presented with the concept of integrity of membership noted above, a new member's response might well be, "That is exactly what I'm looking for." A policy of creating committed members will signal the beginning of a new era for your congregation.

## The extraordinary power of the membership committee

Throughout this book I mention repeatedly that church leaders create a congregation in their own image. Confident leadership will create a congregation of empowered people. Weak leadership will create a congregation of timid souls. This concept is especially applicable to the membership committee.

> *The membership committee should be comprised of people who believe Unitarian Universalism has changed their lives for the better, and who will express their convictions to potential new members.*

Being on the membership committee is a powerful calling, a special ministry. It is not just another committee assignment. Only committed members who believe the church has had a consequential impact on their lives should serve in this important capacity. In addition, only committed members who embrace the concept of integrity of membership noted above should serve on the membership committee.

The makeup of the membership committee is critical because this committee wields considerable influence in shaping new members' attitudes toward the church. Membership is the "front line" of the congregation. Membership sets the standard. People who serve on the membership committee should be hearty, outgoing, enthusiastic, vigorous souls who believe the church is the greatest thing since sliced bread.

The membership committee is not the place for extremely shy, introverted souls who are ill at ease meeting new people. Nor is the membership committee (or any committee for that matter) the place for people who believe that members cannot be asked to do much, that times are tough and UUs can't be asked to increase their charitable giving, and that people can be fringe members or remain uncommitted friends.

> *UU congregations have both the authority and the responsibility to set standards for membership. Individual members do not set standards for themselves.*

A membership orientation session is an essential requirement for membership, to articulate the church's expectations clearly. This includes UUs who previously belonged to other congregations. Do not allow UUs to transfer bad habits from a former church to yours.

I cringe when I see membership literature that states, "You may participate in all the church's activities and programs without becoming a member." Such statements weaken the meaning of membership, permit people to be observers and not participants in ministry, and suggest that others will pay their way. Membership should be an honor. UU congregations should proudly proclaim, "Membership in this congregation is an exceptional experience. We invite you to share the duties, responsibilities, and privileges of this remarkable community."

UU churches should get out of the low expectation game because low expectations result in limitations on everything a congregation wishes to accomplish. Uncommitted members aid in creating a passive congregation that has no clear focus, few core values, and little confidence to embark on new initiatives. Uncommitted people on the membership committee will exacerbate this unfortunate situation.

Let's take a closer look at each of the elements that constitute integrity of membership, to determine if they are, in fact, reasonable or not.

## Attend Sunday services regularly

I'm taken aback at how many UU congregations do not encourage regular attendance at Sunday services. Small miracles occur in church every Sunday, and if building community is a primary goal of congregational life, members need to gather regularly. All too often the UU message is pantheistic, that a walk in the woods or a stroll on the beach is comparable to being in community with fellow congregants. As noted, only about half of UUs attend Sunday services regularly. How do we convince potential new members that church is important if half the current members don't show up?

The membership materials of a theologically liberal Congregational church state, "If you are ill or out of town, you are excused from Sunday services. Otherwise, we expect you to be here." When I mentioned this to a group of UUs some months later, one person scoffed and said, "Sunday attendance is a guilt trip, a Catholic anachronism." But another person said, "Sunday attendance is vital. If church members are out of town, they should attend services in the city they are visiting, either a UU church or one of another denomination." Where is your congregation located on this spectrum of religious practice? Attitudes are of great consequence. They shape our religious identity and the value we attach to it.

I grew up near a stately Catholic church, built in the 1800s. Attached to the first three pews are brass plaques that read, "Reserved for the sick." Even being sick is no excuse from not showing up on Sunday!

Sunday should be the first day of the week, a day of new beginnings. Each week should begin on a high note by going to church. This is the legacy we should pass down to our children and grandchildren, a faith with meaning, purpose, and importance.

## Participate in one program each year that deepens your faith

Many UU churches offer a plethora of programs, frequently led by members who have an interest in a particular subject. Examples include the writings of Walt Whitman, a class on the environment, a journal writing class, or a book discussion group. These programs have a certain benefit, as they draw people together. But programs and classes on secular topics do not help UUs delve more deeply into religious teachings and the insight they provide. I recommend that UU congregations include distinctly religious subjects in 75 percent of their programming. Looking to our own heritage, programs may include the writings of our forbearers William Ellery Channing and Hosea Ballou; or the history of female circuit-riding Unitarian ministers of the 1800s, who founded new churches across the Midwest. Classes may also be contemporary in nature, such as the meteoric rise of nondenominational churches, including a visit to such a church. UUs find the writings of radical Episcopal Bishop John Shelby Spong to be particularly provocative. Bible studies in UU congregations attract sizable audiences. The array of religious topics is endless.

Such courses and programs should also extend beyond the introductory level. Churches of all faiths now present cumulative programs that go beyond "Church 101." It may be necessary to engage speakers or course leaders outside your congregation to add this needed depth. The following chapter, *Focus on What is Important*, expands on this concept as the essential ingredient in creating strong and vital congregations.

Religious insight should not come only from the pulpit. UUs bear the responsibility to become highly literate religious citizens who are eloquent about the UU faith and can assist others in determining their own religious journeys.

### Participate in one outreach or mission project each year beyond the church's four walls

I urge clergy, lay leaders, and people in the pews to consider service to others as the culmination of life in UU communities. This goal includes congregants of all theological persuasions. The key elements of congregational life such as membership, worship, fellowship, stewardship, and learning do not stand in isolation from one another. Rather, they should lead members to service. Congregations need direction. Members need direction. That direction is service to the larger world. It's all about movement, helping members grow in faith, not permitting them to settle into a comfortable, unchallenging routine. Whatever struggles UUs encounter in their own lives, other people are worse off.

In my experience, less than 10 percent of the members of UU congregations nationwide are involved in some outreach or service capacity. If our congregations are to assume more meaningful roles in society, membership involvement needs to increase exponentially.

## Reach the 5 to 10 percent charitable giving level as soon as possible

I make the case for increased giving in Chapter 6, *Making the Annual Pledge Drive Obsolete.* Especially notable is that middle class Americans could double their charitable giving to all causes and not notice the slightest difference in their daily lives. Thus, UU congregations could double their annual pledge drives with ease.

I recall working with a relatively upscale UU congregation in New England. Part of our work together was a session with board members and committee chairs, about 25 people in all. I was surprised that the sexton and his wife were in attendance. They lived in a small, church-owned house on the grounds, and did minor repairs and housekeeping. This couple was in their 50s but looked much older. It appeared as though life had not been kind to them for a good long while.

The subject of charitable giving was on the agenda, and I introduced the idea that members and friends could be asked to commit five percent of their incomes to the church. To my surprise, a number of church leaders argued strenuously that five percent was considerably beyond what members could afford.

The sexton's wife raised her hand guardedly and said that she and her husband belonged to a nearby Episcopal church, and they gave 10 percent of their income to that congregation. They had done this for as long as she could remember. It was how they lived their beliefs, sharing with those who were less fortunate. A silence came over the room. It was obvious that these two people were the poorest in the group. They earned little. They gave much. They were a great inspiration.

I believe we should be increasingly generous because that's the kind of people UUs should strive to be, as we inhabit this earth each day.

At the congregational level, low or nonexistent expectations of charitable giving create perennial budget struggles. Little new territory can be explored, and few people outside the church hear the good news, or are helped to lead more meaningful lives.

From time to time, UUs tell me that upon encountering sorrow and injustice in the world, they feel helpless. Surely, helplessness cannot be the prevailing sentiment of life in UU congregations. In my experience, UU congregations have all the resources imaginable to accomplish anything they set their minds to.

## Tell others about the church

Evangelism is the great stumbling block of liberal religion. UUs would never push their beliefs onto others. Doing so would be déclassé, bad form. But there is a difference between strident evangelism and a heartfelt sharing of one's religious convictions.

Evangelism in UU circles varies from generation to generation. Younger churchgoers are quite comfortable talking about church with others. Their view is that if something in their lives is important, why wouldn't they tell others about it? The purpose in talking about Unitarian Universalism is not necessarily to convince other people to become UUs, but rather to suggest that a life of faith is rich in meaning and purpose. Countless surveys indicate that people who go to church are happier and live longer. Is sharing a heartfelt belief really that difficult?

## Is membership growth a desirable goal?

For some readers, this may be a surprising question. Do UU congregations actually wish to grow in membership? Many congregations claim they would like to grow, but little effort ensues. More than one church author has noted that congregations claim they wish to grow, but nobody wants all those strangers around here!

Membership committees in liberal congregations tend to prefer doing what is familiar rather than making the necessary changes to attract and retain new members. And in my experience, changing an unproductive membership program is a superhuman task. The greatest hurdles are the ingrained belief that potential new members will find the church on their own, and that the congregation is impotent in its ability to grow its own ranks.

We also need to acknowledge that UU congregations often contain people or groups who do not want the church to grow. These groups tend to believe the church should care for current members rather than be concerned with others. This is the "church as private club" mentality. While these groups may be small and reflect a minority opinion, they nevertheless can create an attitude of unfriendliness in a congregation, especially a smaller one.

A significant reason for a lackadaisical or even hostile attitude toward growth stems from UU congregations having little or no interest in reaching people who are lost and lonely. In my work with congregations, I urge those present who discovered the church at an uncertain point in their own lives to take on this extremely valuable ministry, to bring wandering souls into community.

I also appeal to readers of this book who fit this description to come forward and take up this ministry that could make such a difference in the lives of so many. Bringing in new people and welcoming them to the congregation is one of the most valuable and heartening roles a church can offer.

CHAPTER 5

# Focus on Things that Are Important

*We challenge people to lead the religious life.*
*We don't welcome spectators.*
— Rev. Dan Yeary, minister of the 7,000-member North Phoenix Baptist Church, whose congregants include John McCain

*I find a great spiritual hunger among many people who are uncomfortable with talk of God, let alone the idea of church.*
— Author Kathleen Norris

This chapter is about how UU congregations can become more influential in their communities and in the larger world. Isn't this an appealing aspiration? Wouldn't you be thrilled to a member of a congregation that is known for something extraordinarily important?

UU congregations should continually strive for a greater sphere of influence. Why not? UUs are intelligent, well educated, entrepreneurial, and like to get new things going, don't they? Shouldn't Unitarian Universalism be an overflowing wellspring of progressive religion?

Expanding the church's influence, an extraordinarily commendable objective, does not depend on how much money a particular congregation has. Rather, congregations that desire a stronger presence in their communities will find that possible through the membership's collective journey toward spiritual maturity. This is a journey upon which all members can be embarked, regardless of theology.

Skeptical readers may be wary of an emphasis on the spiritual life. I recall one UU minister saying, "We survived spirituality in the 1980s. We can survive it again!"

Before proceeding, we should consider a rudimentary definition of spirituality, as contrasted to spiritual maturity. In reviewing many church websites and newsletters, my impression of UU spirituality is that it's mainly a topic of discussion groups. Classes are a few weeks in length, and gather people together to share their views.

There is value in these gatherings, though classes of this nature appear to be rudimentary in nature. They don't seem to require any reading or preparation. Nor do they appear to require any follow-up. People just get together and talk. I'm not suggesting these conversations are uninteresting. But I do suggest that such conversations have little to do with the congregation achieving its rightful purpose.

Classes of this nature appear to focus on members developing a personal spirituality, one that works for them as individuals. Does this mean that in a congregation of 150 members, 250 members, or 1,000 members, the goal is to develop a respective number of individual characterizations of spirituality? I'm trying to conjure up what hundreds of different spiritualities might look like. It reminds me of the cowboy who jumped on his horse and rode off in all directions. Is this how UU congregations build community or shared ministry?

I'm not suggesting that UUs march in lockstep to a limited definition of the spiritual life, like fundamentalists. Rather, I believe the spiritual life should encompass core values that UUs share in common, that bind people together in shared purpose.

Now let's consider spiritual maturity, another matter altogether. The late William Sloane Coffin said that courage is the first virtue, from which all other virtues emanate. Progressive churches seize on this concept. They believe that if congregants achieve spiritual maturity, all things become possible. All things! Therein lies the true power of a community of faith.

The issue of courage arises in *Gilead*, a Pulitzer Prize winning book by Marilynne Robinson. This stunning novel takes the form of a memoir, written by a Congregational minister to his young son. In the book, the minister writes about his grandfather, also a minister. He writes:

> *My grandfather had nowhere to spend his courage, no way to feel it in himself. This was a great pity.*[1]

In congregational life today, I wonder if we encourage people to spend their courage; or to find it in themselves, if they feel courage is lacking. Churches tend to follow the familiar path, and too easily settle into a routine. I remember a newly settled minister commenting, "I feel like I'm driving in someone else's ruts."

But St. John of the Cross wrote that people who seek God will follow a familiar path, but that path will end, and there will be no path. This is my hope and dream for UU congregations across the land, that the familiar path will end, and that members will find themselves in uncharted territory. In fact, I believe UU congregations intentionally need to venture there.

Let me provide a few examples. I recall working with an Episcopal congregation in Vancouver, British Columbia. Some years before, about 15 church members had participated in a two-year spiritual maturity class. Can you imagine a church asking people to make a two-year commitment?

The first year involved weekly Bible study, along with reading ancient and contemporary theologians. Homework was required. The group also met for occasional meals and two weekend retreats. This class was not easy. It required a significant commitment of time and effort. The second year was to involve some type of outward ministry. The minister who led this program believed that achieving substantial good in the world required a solid spiritual foundation.

During this two-year class, preparations for the upcoming Olympics were underway in the Vancouver area. With hordes of people coming to town, adequate housing was a key issue. The members of the class were distressed to learn that hundreds of elderly people who lived in low-income, residential hotels in the downtown area were to be relocated to scattered suburban locales.

The participants in this class believed that moving elderly residents to faraway neighborhoods was an egregious policy. Many elderly people had lived downtown for years. This was their community. The class took on this issue as their outward ministry. Not a single person in the group had any experience in housing, gerontology, or issues of large-scale public policy.

To make a long story short, when I visited Vancouver I was given a tour of three downtown buildings the church owned (through a nonprofit organization it founded) that housed 435 elderly residents. I met three members of the original class, who told me their faith sustained them through years of hard work and the difficulties they encountered in making their dream come true – reading hundreds of documents; making scores of phone calls and appointments; having scores of phone calls unreturned and appointments cancelled; the obstacles and setbacks; the many attempts to find sufficient money to fund the project; the legal challenges; and the time, energy, and stamina required to enlist hundreds of people in the project, sway public opinion, and stay the course.

To a person, they claimed they would never have had the courage or the determination to make such a time-consuming commitment without a solid grounding in their faith. These people took on, and accomplished, holy work. All things became possible.

Readers of a certain age will recognize the second example, that of the Berrigan brothers. Even after being jailed for burning draft records in 1968, these two Catholic priests and six other activists gained access to the General Electric nuclear missile site in King of Prussia, Pennsylvania, in 1980, where they poured their own blood on nuclear warheads. Even readers who believe these were foolhardy acts would grudgingly admit this civil disobedience required an extraordinary level of courage.

Before any such attempt, the Berrigans and their fellow activists met in retreat. For ten days to two weeks, they would read, study, discuss, and pray about what they intended to do. Only when they felt spiritually prepared would they proceed.

Of course, the life of Dr. Martin Luther King, Jr. is a superb example of courage that comes from a profoundly deep faith.

At the congregational level, I have met courageous UUs who have adopted minority children, served as foster parents, and founded orphanages. I've met UUs who have given extraordinary amounts of money to worthy causes, money they sometimes didn't have. I've met and worked with dedicated church members who devoted thousands of hours year after year in community gardens that grow vegetables for local food banks.

I've also known church people who have encountered debilitating illness and tragedy, and have endured it with a gracefulness beyond my own comprehension. I've known UUs who took financial risks by leading capital campaigns for their congregations for renovations and new construction because they foresaw a brighter future. I have also met UUs who have stood on the front lines of social action initiatives in their home communities. I have met UUs who made sacrifices in their personal lives for the greater good.

This is what spiritual maturity looks like – the courage to act on our principles. This courage crosses all theological lines. I believe such courage is more likely to occur among people in a faith community than individuals acting on their own.

This is our goal, to develop the strength to become effective in our roles, no matter how overwhelming or how insignificant certain tasks appear to be at the time. In doing so, we know with great assurance that our faith and our faith community will be staunch allies.

## The essential question

These heroic people raise the question, "What is the purpose of the church? What should we be about?" The answer is unexpectedly simple. Schools educate students. Widget manufacturers make widgets. The purpose of the church is to develop spiritually mature members. This is our "product line," people who find within themselves the courage, fortitude, and stamina to stake out better lives for themselves, their families, and their fellow citizens. Unitarian Universalism should not be a religious movement for fringe members, spectators, or the uncommitted.

Developing spiritually mature members will not happen with people sitting in groups, talking and listening. Right living is more the challenge than right thinking.

Enlightened reason, the hallowed tradition that supports much UU church programming, is insufficient in creating a spiritually mature congregation. Enlightened reason does not define a collective path that a congregation might travel together. UU minister Paul Hull correctly states, "Unitarian Universalism should drop its emphasis on enlightened reason and substitute an affirmation of how people find true meaning in their lives."

## Heady stuff

Some readers may feel a bit unsettled with my description of a committed Unitarian Universalist being one who is on a journey toward spiritual maturity. They may be thinking, "The church shouldn't define the spiritual life for me. I can do that on my own, or not do that if I please." Humanists and atheists may be thinking that the spiritual life is too "religious" and holds little interest for them.

In addition, people lead busy lives these days. They have many obligations. How could they possibly find time to develop a spiritual life?

We should be honest with ourselves and admit that as a low expectation movement, UU churches ask very little of us. A colleague of mine often says, "A lot of churches motivate people to go home and have lunch." We have made membership too easy, too comfortable, too convenient.

Many church members may perceive no need for the congregation to seek a future that is appreciably different from today. If current members are content and little urgency exists about issues of congregational life, things as they are will proceed for a good long while. This state of affairs is satisfying to some and maddening to others.

In many congregations, members enjoy the preaching, the music, the fellowship, the coffee, the church's programs, their kid's Sunday school, participating in a book discussion group, and being part of a short-term outreach project from time to time. Preferably, all this doesn't cost very much and isn't too inconvenient. The church meets their needs. For many, this constitutes the essential UU church. Why change something that people find comfortable?

For congregations that have little motivation to widen their vision or challenge members to a higher calling, the fundamental question becomes whether contentment is a valid goal. UU minister Julie-Ann Silberman-Bunn believes that hotels and day spas are in the satisfaction business, but congregations are not. She writes,

> *A church is not a place where you are catered to and pampered. Our congregations are religious communities, sanctuaries for those in need, safe havens, and respites from the chaos of the world. Churches neither expect nor guarantee your satisfaction.*[2]

She further suggests that people harbor a misunderstanding of religious life. They come into churches and sit down in the same manner as they enter restaurants or concert halls, like spectators coming to enjoy what is prepared for them, what is served up for their senses. Thus, many do not understand the complex requirements of being a valued participant in a community of faith.

Paul Wilkes, author of the superb book, *Excellent Protestant Congregations*, believes that church communities should be pushed to the edge of their comfort zones. Congregations should also be called to do things they think they cannot do.[3] Collective accomplishment is a critical factor in creating healthy communities of all types. In the church world, such efforts give rise to congregations that perceive a higher purpose, which in turn, lessens the priority on individual satisfaction.

> *We should demand a faith that asks something of us, not settle for one that requires very little.*

## The entryway to what is important

Any congregation wishing to create a greater dimension for itself requires one of two things: either dissatisfaction with some aspect of church life, or a collective yearning for a greater purpose and engagement with the world.

Dissatisfaction and yearning take many forms. For example, one UU congregation had a large endowment but minimal outreach. A growing number of members felt strongly that being inward-focused was the opposite of what they wished to church to be. They came to the realization that they inhabited a private enclave far removed from the needs of their community.

Another congregation perceived its programs as remaining similar year to year, and was experiencing staleness in congregational life. The members of another UU church told me the congregation had a moderate case of depression. This was visible in a joyless worship service and in the subdued coffee hour that followed. Sadly, this particular congregation had little reason for being. Finally, I've worked with many medium-sized and large congregations that function like small churches. In these instances, clergy and lay leaders believed their inherent potential was underutilized, that much good work was going undone.

These examples illustrate an understandable need for revitalization, a redefining of what the congregation is called to do in this place and time. In my view, this redefinition should result in a congregation with a clearly defined purpose, a congregation that is on a shared religious journey.

A Lutheran minister once noted that the purpose of a church is not to bring people into the building and "cage" them in programs. The purpose of a church is to empower people, challenge them to lead more purposeful lives, and provide them the courage to make the world a better place in which to live.

Therein lies the difference between the traditional church and the progressive church. It's not a matter of a liberal or conservative theology. Rather, the litmus test is people becoming different from who they once were.

> *It's also about people coming to realize that developing a spiritual life is worth the time and effort, to seek a life of greater meaning and purpose.*

The North Phoenix Baptist church mentioned in the introductory quote takes a four-pronged strategy in accomplishing this goal. Three of the four are externally oriented, and include:

- To connect with the community in meaningful relationship
- To commit to making a difference in the world
- To engage our world through life patterns and life systems

These three primary goals are non-theological in content. They would appeal to people in many faith traditions, including Unitarian Universalism. The fourth, as expected in a Christian setting, is to celebrate the love that God provides.[4]

I was particularly struck with the third statement, to engage our world through life patterns and life systems. This extraordinarily progressive church expects people to reconsider the way they live their daily lives, to live together faithfully in community. This concept is another essential key to stronger UU congregations and congregants alike. I believe this is what people yearn for.

## Getting closer to the things that are important

In most congregations, the only consistent opportunity to serve is in the management of the church itself. The nominating committee perennially seeks volunteers to chair various committees and take up myriad assignments that keep the church functioning month to month.[5]

Unfortunately, a primary emphasis on institutional maintenance detracts from a congregation determining its true role and purpose.

## Who are UUs anyway, and do they want a spiritual life?

At one time, I belonged to a UU congregation in an affluent community that is representative of many in the US. I was astonished at the number of extraordinarily well-educated, successful people who gathered in this church. I had never experienced such a concentration of doctors, lawyers, academics, writers, consultants, bankers, patent holders, and entrepreneurs in my life.

Many church members owned vacation homes, traveled abroad, and sent their kids to private schools. The choir boasted four paid soloists and the music was divine. Church receptions featured homegrown strawberries and fine wines. All was right with the world. This seemed to be a church for people who didn't need church. They lived extraordinarily rich lives. What could Unitarian Universalism, or any religion for that matter, provide that they didn't already have?

It wasn't until months and sometimes years later that I discovered parishioners had lost jobs, struggled with finances, fought serious illness, were raising children with learning disabilities, and dealt with extraordinarily difficult family concerns. I was astonished that church members could leave the struggles of their lives at home and preserve a high level of decorum at church. Members' concerns were unseen and unspoken, other than to the minister in private conversation, if that.

I realize many people wish to keep family matters private. This is certainly understandable. At the same time, I often speak with people who left churches of many faiths because they felt the congregation abandoned them in time of need.

I shared these thoughts with a UU minister who has served as interim minister for half a dozen churches over the past few years. He responded,

> *My congregants are suffering from a host of anxieties, illnesses, financial crises, children on drugs, relatives in prison, lost jobs, the meaninglessness and emptiness brought on by consumerism and mass media, parents needing constant care one minute and grandchildren the next. Despite all this, my congregants devote sizable chunks of their time and money to helping those less fortunate. Meanwhile, the denominational powers and church structures do little or nothing to address the real pastoral needs of our people.*

Herein lies the purpose of a church, what is truly important, and the difference between the traditional church and the progressive church. The traditional UU church is based on information-oriented classes and programs, usually offered at an introductory level. Wayne Rhodes, a former Marine officer and Presbyterian minister, says, "The program model of ministry does not help congregants build a deep faith or face life's challenges. It creates congregations that deal mainly with surface issues."

To me, Rhodes's view resonates powerfully. In my experience with UU and Protestant churches, I have found that most congregations rarely progress beyond surface issues. I believe this is why millions of people abandoned traditional churches. There is little substance to be found.

This returns us to the progressive church, and what it has to offer. In their book, *Simple Church*, authors Rainer and Geiger raise this very issue.

Many churches, they claim, are over-programmed and busyness is the norm. Church calendars are cluttered with multiple events that address a multiplicity of topics. But there is no clear beginning or end, only an assortment of programs. There is no big picture, no particular direction.

In contrast, the simple church shapes its classes and programs to produce a life-changing faith that moves congregants steadily along a path toward spiritual maturity. These churches reject the "menu" philosophy of adding ever more unconnected programs.

> *The emphasis is on creating an environment that helps people grow ever deeper in faith, strengthen their ability to enhance their own lives, deal with life's difficulties, and improve the lives of others.*[6]

## Traveling the journey is what's important

The church environment that lends itself to spiritual growth of its members is based on a straightforward premise:

> *Congregants always know what the next step in the journey will be.*

Simple churches continually ask, "What does a spiritually mature person look like?" Spiritually mature people attend Sunday services regularly, to understand God more fully. (UUs can make the translation here.) Members participate regularly in small groups, to know and understand one another. Church members also participate in ministries that impact others. These are the three standards for all members of the congregation.

While not exactly mandatory, these standards are also not optional. Potential members are told that if they do not perceive themselves traveling this journey, this is not their church. Being a spectator is not an option.

In congregations like this, the spiritual lives of members are continually assessed. Members are asked, "Are you learning to know and understand God?" If not, church members are guided toward someone or some resource that will help them overcome that obstacle.

Members are also asked, "Are you getting to know others in the church through small groups?" This is a prerequisite for reaching out to the larger world. And, members are asked, "Are you involved in a ministry that serves those in need?" No matter where congregants are on their journeys, they always know what the next step is, and who will be there to guide them.

It's not that church members keep a spiritual report card and are called to task if they fall short. (However, I am familiar with churches in which members locate spiritual partners, and each week they exchange written summaries of how their spiritual lives have progressed, or not progressed during that time.) Rather, like trying to lose weight or quit smoking, people are more likely to achieve their goals if they work together in community. Any type of group initiative is also more effective if accountability is a key ingredient. Good intentions do not suffice.

This ongoing and continual assessment of a church member's spiritual journey stands in contrast to traditional churches that measure success by attendance at church events. For example, if 20 people attend a book discussion group, this would be viewed as a success in most churches. Few ask if this program connects to any others in a recognizable sequence, leads to a member's deeper understanding of the faith, or fulfills the congregation's true purpose.

In looking at church websites, one UU congregation listed 62 programs over the course of a four-month period. This is an impressive array. They are very busy. But what is the point if a random assortment of members attends the art fair, participates in the bike ride, or gathers to discuss marriage equality? To be fair, some programs are about Unitarian Universalism and issues like reaching out to others. But these are a distinct minority compared to social events and information-based classes on secular topics.

And, of course, all programs on this church's calendar are optional. People may or may not attend, so this programming does not promote a meaningful congregational involvement, something that all members share in common.

Progressive churches, both liberal and conservative, proclaim, "This is who we are and what we teach." These churches are based on the human life cycle and the real-life concerns that people, both inside and outside the church, face every day.

> *Helping people lead purposeful lives and assisting others to do likewise is focusing on things that are important. We are each other's keepers.*

Worship services in progressive churches include frequent references that all people suffer, and none are immune. This is not just an acknowledgement that suffering exists, but also that the church stands ready to help. Church members who have experienced similar difficulties are present to assist others along life's difficult paths. The rise of the program called Stephen Ministries, which trains lay people to be competent listeners to those experiencing difficulty, attests to this fact. The church exists to provide people with hope for the future, to make their burdens light. This is not church as group therapy. Rather, church is an entity that helps people find solutions to life's most pressing concerns.

### Is the path to spiritual maturity possible?

The jury is out on whether UU congregations will discard their emphasis on information-based classes and substitute a journey toward spiritual maturity instead. Building meaningful lives is what ministry is all about. Constructing purposeful lives is the calling. What kind of people are we called to become, and how do we become those people in community?

Since no UU church to my knowledge has ever challenged an entire congregation to make a commitment to spiritual maturity, the best I can do is offer guidelines rather than tried-and-true experience. But I believe there is ample evidence that hearty souls can give it a try, with a reasonable chance of success. Here's how.

In my book *The Almost Church*, I wrote that UUs from coast to coast have powerful yearnings for what their churches might become. These yearnings include:

- *I wish my church had a more significant and visible community impact.*
- *I hope for a willingness of my congregation to live more boldly.*
- *I wish we accomplished great things, or affected lives.*
- *I wish we weren't so well established in the middle of the road.*
- *I yearn for a church where service is the core, and not at the edges.*
- *I wish this church took some risks.*
- *We're too comfortably settled in.*
- *I wish we weren't so penny-pinching, and gave more to the needs of the world.*

These sentiments come from hundreds of UUs across the country. Their heartfelt feelings indicate without doubt that UUs want significantly more from congregational life. They are waiting to be challenged. In particular, I was touched by the person who wrote:

> *I yearn for a church-wide commitment to living the faith.*[7]

These are comments from passionately beating hearts that will lead Unitarian Universalist congregations to create courageous souls who are not satisfied with things as they are. These are people who desire a deeper faith, who wish to set an example for others, and who wish to create a more equitable society.

For a congregation to consider the path to spiritual maturity, these passionately beating hearts must include clergy and lay leaders who themselves will travel this journey. Otherwise, the congregation's journey will be in doubt. For clergy who may be uncertain of this path, numerous surveys of parishioners over the years contain one particular complaint – that ministers too seldom speak like people with a spiritual life of their own, who are living the things they preach. I believe this is a valid criticism.

But options exist. If the leadership of your congregation is not committed to this journey, those who desire a deeper spiritual life can create their own path. Be assured that your journey will not conflict with that of the larger congregation. Quite the contrary, those in your ranks will be a good influence on fellow members. You will be living an unconventional life, a more interesting way of life.

*Do not hold a congregational discussion or vote to decide on whether spiritual maturity should be a primary emphasis!* In any congregation, the number of uncommitted members is larger than the number of committed members, and any initiative that includes higher expectations will be voted down. Uncommitted members should not be permitted to make this important decision for others.

Even if all the stars line up and the leadership is on board, the process I'm describing will require a three to five year period, perhaps longer. There are no quick fixes. Be patient. I know of a prominent church consultant who will not sign a contract with a congregation for less than a three-year period. It takes time for a congregation to assume a new or different reason for being.

If the leadership wishes to enhance the congregation's spiritual maturity, an excellent place to begin is introducing the concept to new members. This means the membership committee needs to be on board. If the membership committee is not, the leadership should reconstitute the membership committee with people who are.

In Chapter Four, we discussed integrity of membership. This is an excellent starting point for a journey toward spiritual maturity. (Attend services regularly. Participate in one program each year that deepens your faith. Participate in one outreach ministry. Strive to reach the 5 to 10 percent giving level. Tell others about the church.)

Beyond these essentials of membership, I don't believe UUs in any congregation who wish to achieve spiritual maturity can just think it up on their own. People need a greater breadth of knowledge and some guidelines in how to craft the spiritual life. Discussion groups alone are not sufficient.

## Recommendations on getting started

Those familiar with Scripture might find the following guidelines similar to the Book of Deuteronomy, in which the various commandments and judgments are laid out. Great rewards follow those who adhere to the statutes. "Blessed shalt thou be when thou comest in, and blessed shalt thou be when thou goest out." (Deuteronomy 28:6) That sounds good to me.

Speaking of Scripture, even a brief review of literature on the spiritual life turns up the word *discipline* frequently. For many, the word *discipline* sends up red flags. They believe it can only refer to a joyless routine that will burden their already over-scheduled lives. However, discipline in the congregational context is a means to a joyful, rich life. Many wondrous things in life require a certain discipline – learning to play a musical instrument, learning to waltz, learning a foreign language, reading serious literature, maintaining a healthy diet, regular exercise. Discipline in congregational life is not something that UUs need fear.

Church literature often suggests a number of disciplines around which the spiritual life may be achieved. These include the disciplines of:

Meditation, reflection, or prayer
Study
Simplicity
Fasting
Solitude
Service
Admission of one's weaknesses and a desire to do better
Worship
Guidance
Forgiveness
Celebration

You may certainly add others to this list.

The following are a summary of attitudes and beliefs, the "qualifications," so to speak, of those who wish to travel the journey to a mature spiritual life. Some have been mentioned earlier in this chapter and elsewhere in the book, but it will be helpful to summarize them all together, for ease of reference.

- Those seeking a deeper faith will need to make a commitment to achieving this goal, perhaps a lifelong commitment. Faith development is a process that grows ever deeper and richer. Peter Gomes, Minister of Harvard's Memorial Church, once spoke about reviewing his sermons from 20 years prior, and being struck with how wrong he felt himself to be at the time. He believed that continued study helped evolve in his faith and understanding of the human condition over time. He felt this was an exiting process of discovery, a life worth living in whatever context one finds one's self.

- The disciplines of reading and study will reveal how others have built life-sustaining, spiritual lives. I've included some excellent references in Appendix A. Included in your readings should be James Fowler's book, *Stages of Faith*.[8] Fowler's book is the seminal study in an individual's faith journey from simple understanding to an enlightened state.

- Regardless of theology, a prerequisite for spiritual maturity must include some refutation of the consumer society in which we live. This is the discipline of simplicity. Ever-longer work weeks, ever larger houses financed with ever-greater amounts of debt, and acquiring ever more expensive consumer goods are not the pinnacle of American life; for church members, their children, or their grandchildren. A major challenge is to redefine what the proverbial "good life" actually is.

  In her book, *Dakota: A Spiritual Geography*, Kathleen Norris describes moving from New York City to Lemmon, South Dakota, population 1,600. She explains that she does not feel deprived, living in a small rural community. She writes, "Surrendering to reduced circumstances enhances the whole person. It is a radical way of knowing exactly who, what, and where you are, in defiance of those powerful forces in society – alcohol, drugs, television, shopping malls – that aim to make us forget.[9]

- Participants in the journey are encouraged to reach the 5 to 10 percent charitable giving level as soon as possible.
- People might consider a largely vegetarian diet, as many acres of arable land and huge amounts of water and feed are required to produce livestock.
- Participants are encouraged to maintain some type of Sabbath, one day per week set aside for rest, reflection, and contemplation.
- Participants need to gather regularly. I encourage interested readers to consider a few times monthly at a minimum. All participants need to be committed to mutual goals. Your work together is not a discussion group, but a commitment to a defined way of life. You may certainly invite occasional visitors, but this is not the place for perpetual observers or uncommitted souls.
- Participants might consider turning off their television sets much of the time, and getting rid of their TV sets altogether. A friend of mine, with a wife and two teenagers, rents a television during the Olympics and the World Series. During the week or so the rental TV is in the house, his kids can watch anything they want, for as long as they want. He claims that after a week, his kids are clamoring to get that TV out of the house. It can happen. Doing so will spare yourselves and your children a great deal of gratuitous sex, violence, and relentless advertising. I recall a UU mom saying her 11-year old daughter's favorite show was Sex and the City. Could not owning a TV be worse than this? When my own kids were growing up, we didn't have a TV for nine years. They turned out OK.
- Participants would find great meaning in ministry or community service beyond the church's four walls. One doesn't need to look far to find people in need.
- People who embark on this journey may need help beyond their own ranks, in the form of others who can lead groups toward their goal. This might involve people from other faith traditions. One of the most deeply spiritual people I've ever met is an Episcopalian deacon, a woman who lives a life that includes periods of silence and trips to Haiti to work in a hospital for the poor. Sometimes

people who live this life are trained as spiritual directors, and work with both individuals and groups.

- Your group must always be open to newcomers who commit to the journey, and cannot become "closed" in any way, shape, or form. If a group becomes too large, and wouldn't that be wonderful, break into smaller groups but insist on member rotation. Groups should not maintain consistent membership for months and years on end. Doing so is antithetical to a shared religious journey for the congregation as a whole.

Beyond these guidelines, I do not have a tried-and-true method for spiritual maturity to share with readers. You may pick and choose from these suggestions, or create your own. Many paths are possible. The bottom line concept, however, is a life with some self-limitation.

My belief is that people who yearn for a deeper spiritual life, and who find the above guidelines appealing, will find compelling ways to reach their goals. If I lived in your town, I would join a group like this in the blink of an eye.

CHAPTER 6

# Making the Annual Pledge Drive Obsolete

*Charity is enjoined upon each of us, not simply upon the rich, or upon those who can be said to afford it.*
— Rev. Peter Gomes
Memorial Church, Harvard University

*One of the most boring things to do with money is just spend it.*
— Robert W. Wilson, a successful investor who lives frugally and plans to give away his entire $800 million fortune

Making the annual pledge drive obsolete is based on four principles:

- Pledge drives ultimately rest on the transformative power of Unitarian Universalism to help us lead more purposeful lives. In my view, this transformative power is waiting to be tapped.
- The responsibility for a successful pledge drive does not rest with the Stewardship Committee. Success in the stewardship realm is the responsibility of the minister(s), board members, and lay leaders of the congregation. The Stewardship Committee only conveys their message of hope for the future.
- Middle class Americans could double their charitable giving to all causes and not notice the slightest difference in their daily lives. Thus, UU congregations could double their annual pledge drives with ease. The money is out there. UU churches should be in the business of creating philanthropists, one of life's most noble and highest callings. We just haven't convinced people that giving away money is fun! Surely, being a generous person or family is one of

life's great privileges. Aren't we privileged to be part of a community that can create a more just and humane world?

- The time, effort, and angst invested in the annual pledge drive are exceedingly poor investments of the church's resources.

Let's take a look at each issue in turn, along with a few others, including how much UUs can be asked to give.

## The transformative power of Unitarian Universalism

Robert Wuthnow is Director of the Center for the Study of American Religion at Princeton University. His work is highly regarded, including his books about money in the church. His words will resonate with those who desire the church to speak with a more powerful voice and have a greater influence in the world. He writes,

> *Clergy lament the materialism of our society and the pressures to work harder and spend more. They worry that young people are being corrupted by false and misleading values of the marketplace. They acknowledge that wealth and generosity do not go hand in hand. Most clergy realize there is theological support for these opinions. Still, they find it hard to say anything that might seem to criticize the ways their parishioners are living.*[1]

UCC minister Anthony Robinson states it more uncompromisingly, saying that, "People need to detoxify from a culture that is toxic in its materialism, individualism, and violence. The church needs new attitudes, new relationships, new practices, and new perspectives."[2] As a Christian minister, Robinson says that people need to find God.

I believe UU congregations hold the authority to set standards that guide our behavior as people of faith. This authority should be at its zenith in challenging UUs to reject the materialistic society in which we live. The church should take a strong position against the conviction that life is always about having more. Theologian Walter Bruggeman defines this as, "The frantic effort to acquire more – more body surgery, more cosmetics, more cars, more beer, more sex, more certitude, more security, more power, more oil, more whatever."[3]

Challenging the prevailing consumer culture is a powerful way that Unitarian Universalism can and should change our attitudes, our perspectives, and the way we lead our lives. The proverbial good life should not be about acquisition, but rather an innate sense of simplicity, of goodness, of limitation.

Shunning materialistic values goes beyond our individual and family lives, and can serve as a beacon for liberal religion, as well. Wuthnow writes, "Instead of being a reaction to fundamentalism, liberal religion needs to become a counterculture to secularism. [Liberal religion] should present itself as a third way."[4]

Congregations of any faith that wish to confront materialism in their ranks face monumental challenges. The greatest challenge is overcoming the middle class obsession with money and careers. Once people achieve a certain standard of living, they guard it carefully. It is not socially acceptable to consider a lesser standard. Who among us wishes to live in smaller houses, in less desirable neighborhoods, or drive less expensive cars? What would people think?

All too often, we live in a society that assigns status to people according to what they can buy. It's akin to the Calvinist notion of predestination. Successful people must be the elect, those identified by God, who will achieve eternal salvation. Economic instability is associated with moral failure, even today.

"Respectability is the hallmark of the middle class church," Wuthnow writes, "and the tokens of respectability include fine dress, attractive transportation, capacious homes, well-educated children, and successful careers."[5]

When I belonged to the aforementioned affluent New England congregation, I received numerous invitations from church members to visit their homes. These were not strictly social events, nor were they gatherings to discuss the work of the church. Rather, these get-togethers were intended to show off expensive home additions and renovations, including new kitchens with imported granite countertops, family rooms with wide screen TV's and surround sound systems, and spacious master bedrooms with whirlpools in the bathroom and large, walk-in closets. Everyone oohed and ahhed.

In the 1950s novel, *The Man in the Gray Flannel Suit*, fictional character Tom Rath leaves his job at a small foundation to take a higher-paying job at a large corporation. He becomes disillusioned. "I spend my days," he opines, "trying to convince people to eat more corn flakes and smoke more cigarettes and buy more stoves and refrigerators, until they explode with happiness. I do this so I can buy a bigger house and a better brand of gin."

When I observed the huge amounts of money that my fellow congregants had poured into their houses, I wondered if I should have exploded with happiness. Instead, I felt an aching sadness. Are expensive home renovations the pinnacle of American life? Do increasingly frequent trips to the mall constitute life as good as it gets?

Theologians Stanley Hauerwaus and William Willimon phrase the dangers of a consumer mentality in an extremely articulate way. They write,

> *Our society has become a vast supermarket of desire, under the assumption that if we are free enough to choose whatever we want, we can defer eternally the question of what needs are worth having and on what basis right choices are made. What we call "freedom" becomes the tyranny of our own desires.*[6]

Hauerwaus and Willimon fault the contemporary church in not providing an alternative to consumer oriented society in which we live. This is a perfect segue into how charitable UUs might become.

## How much should UUs be asked to give?

A maxim in fund-raising is, "Asking people for money is the easiest way to raise it. All other methods are more difficult." Thus,

> *Clergy and lay leaders should ask members and friends to reach the 5 to 10 percent giving level at the earliest opportunity.*

This level of commitment is increasingly discussed in UU congregations, and is the essential first step in doing away with the annual pledge drive. Members and friends can commit to this level of giving anytime they wish, whenever they decide. Or, they can commit to reaching the 5 to 10 percent level incrementally. No church by-law prohibits people from pledging at any time of year. No one has to wait until the pledge drive rolls around in the fall or spring. Thus, there really doesn't have to be an annual pledge drive, does there? Members and friends can notify the minister or the treasurer of their decision at any time. What could be easier?

Actually, there's a catch. Congregants are unlikely to commit to this level of giving unless clergy, board members, and key lay leaders do likewise. The leadership must set an example for the congregation.

Otherwise, congregational leaders will be asking members to do something they themselves are not.

Giving five to ten percent of one's income is a long-standing tradition in many congregations, of all faiths. I've met many UUs whose parents or grandparents committed 10 percent of their incomes, for decades on end. They could not envision life any other way. These family ancestors were very likely people of lesser means. They set an extraordinary example. Many of them lived by the formula, "Give 10 percent to the church, save 10 percent, and live on the remaining 80 percent." Most American families would be better off financially if they returned to this simple formula.

Invariably, whenever the subject of giving 10 percent arises, someone asks, "Ten percent of gross or net?" I heard a wonderful response to that question recently, from an Episcopalian friend. He said, "Do you want your prayers answered in gross or net terms?"

Especially important in regard to money in family life is the shameless practice of the American advertising industry in targeting younger and younger children. UU congregations need to stand foursquare against the pressure to convince children and youth that life's ultimate cool is to buy ever more fashionable consumer goods.

Many commentators claim that television teaches children values more effectively than any church. This is a sobering thought. Whose values do we wish to impart to our children; the enduring, timeless values of generosity and service offered by the church, or the shallow, fleeting consumer values promoted by ads on television?

One last note on asking people for 5 to 10 percent of their incomes. Some church members may react with "sticker shock." They cannot possibly afford it. They have mortgage payments, car payments, credit card balances, college or private school tuition bills, cable TV and cell phone costs, Internet fees, utility bills, season tickets for the symphony or a professional sports team, and the cost of vacation travel. Some are also paying for housecleaning and landscaping services. Yet others have second homes to pay for, furnish, and maintain. Both husbands and wives work full time and then some to maintain these lifestyles. How could the church possibly ask them to become more charitable? There's just no extra money.

For the moment, let's leave aside the question of whether owning all this stuff represents the good life. When I meet with people who commit 10 percent of their incomes (and sometimes more) to the church or to other causes, I often ask what they gave up to become so generous. To a person, they do not understand the question. The universal response is that they gave up nothing, not a thing. They report their lives have been immeasurably enriched by the experience. Even more surprising, many say they used to worry about finances until they started giving 10 percent, and now that worry has almost completely vanished. This is the great paradox of a religious life. Give it a try and see what happens.

Admittedly, many UUs do not own second homes, travel abroad, or possess the outward trappings that indicate wealth. Their lives, in fact, may be very different. The Federal Reserve Board recently reported that the average American family carries a mortgage of $85,000; car and tuition loans of $14,000; home equity loans of $10,000; and credit card debt of $8,500. That average American family saved $392 the previous year.[7]

If families are overextended, they are in need of financial counseling, which more and more churches now provide. Clergy and lay leaders realize the church will not engage congregants in a meaningful stewardship conversation if people, according to the familiar phrase, are two paychecks away from losing it all.

The church has the power, through its redefinition of the good life and by providing financial counseling services, to assist people in leading better, more fulfilling lives, unencumbered by consumer debt.

We might end this section by considering the Easterlin Paradox, a concept formulated by economist Richard Easterlin. He posits that once people have their basic needs met, they do not become happier as they become richer. (www.wikipedia.com is a good source) Rather, Easterlin's research shows that happiness has less to do with money and more to do with friendships and being involved in causes larger than one's self.

## What about all those poor people in church?

This question often arises in UU congregations when the pledge drive rolls around. I recall a heated conversation in an affluent community (median household income, $110,000) in regard to a proposed $25 membership fee. An extremely vocal group argued that $25 would "price out" many potential members, in addition to being a hardship for some current members.

Another group suggested that congregants be allowed to make five payments of $5 each, to reach the $25 figure, as though members had the incomes of teenage babysitters. The entire conversation was absurd, but demonstrates how deeply the poverty viewpoint is ingrained in some UU congregations.

We need to define who poor people are, to see if they resemble UUs. Most poor people do not own homes and may live in government subsidized housing, are eligible for food stamps, do not have health insurance, and may be unable to afford to take their kids to the dentist. They may not own cars, and rely on public transportation. If they are employed, they labor in menial jobs because they have a high school education at best. They rarely, if ever, go on vacation. If their kids go to college, they most likely attend the local community college and work 25 hours a week or more to afford that. They are likely to live in neighborhoods with higher crime rates than the norm. If your congregation is comprised of people who fit this description, then asking them for money may be a problem.

Likewise, I frequently hear that older people are on fixed incomes, and like poor people, they cannot give much, either. Oddly, people of younger generations are often the ones who make this blanket statement. Of course, some elderly people have limited means. But people 55 and older control approximately 65 percent of all the wealth in America, and many are doing just fine.

It is extremely patronizing for anyone to pass judgment on what other people can or cannot give. Church members are grown-ups. They can make their own decisions regarding their assets and what they wish to share. Clergy and lay leaders are in the business of creating congregations that serve in ever-greater measure. They should not be perceived extracting money from people who don't have it.

## Who's responsible for the success of the pledge drive?

Strong, well-informed leaders will present a continual array of new and captivating ideas that energize a congregation. In churches like this, the pledge drive is built on a year 'round basis of engaging with new people and the wider world.

Most nonprofit organizations operate from this starting point. When you receive mailings from your alma mater, a local hospital, the symphony, or an agency that serves people who are less fortunate, you'll discover there's always something new underway. Nonprofit mailings convey interesting stories and provide donors with innovative and exciting opportunities to give.

I recall working with a congregation that fit this description. In an offhand comment I mentioned that in most churches, running the pledge drive is a thankless task. Shortly thereafter, the entire seven-member stewardship committee mildly admonished me to adjust my attitude. The chairperson said, "We joyfully took on the pledge drive and have every intention of making it successful. This is the best job the church has to offer." She was right. If clergy and lay leaders will not challenge UUs to change the way they lead their lives and work toward making the annual pledge drive obsolete, a stewardship committee of lively souls is the second best scenario.

On a less upbeat note, if the leadership of a church is tentative, hesitant, or takes a maintenance posture, the stewardship committee will be hard-pressed to devise a forward-looking, animated message that convinces the congregation to invest generously in its future. It is just about impossible for a congregation that is complacent eleven months of the year to mount a soul-stirring pledge drive in the twelfth.

In such a situation, the stewardship committee is likely to maintain the status quo, because they have little on which to base the pledge drive. I've worked with more than one congregation that dreaded the pledge drive coming around. Sadly, the opportunity to support the church and its good work is anticipated with a sense of foreboding.

## Let's create some new traditions

We need to leave some old habits behind. The first is same-level giving. The norm in most UU congregations is incremental increases in the annual pledge drive year to year. This is the result of approximately two-thirds of members and friends giving about the same amount, year after year.

The eternal hope is that a more compelling stewardship sermon from the minister or a better-written pledge letter will motivate the masses to give more. This rarely occurs. When increases do occur, they are likely to come from one-third of the membership, those who already give the most.

In my experience, same-level giving among two-thirds of the membership has two particular roots: low expectations of giving when people join; and an ever changing, theme-of-the-year pledge drive. When the church asks people for little in the early going, that's what it will get over the long haul. A new theme each year does not reflect consistent, compelling, long term hopes and dreams for the future. A theme-of-the-year drive is short term in nature, signaling that congregational life is viewed one fiscal year at a time. Themes such as "Living Together in Harmony" are also not forceful enough to help congregants contemplate a more distinctive life together.

## The role of the operating budget

When the pledge drive kicks off, church members are frequently presented with a budget that contains increased costs for personnel, insurance, utilities, and other line items. The key word is "increased." Costs rarely decrease. When next year's budget is rolled out, church members sometimes feel they are being flogged to cover ever-increasing costs.

If costs are up three percent, members may raise their pledges by the same percentage. Thus, a $500 donor might increase to $525, which is actually five percent, but increasing to $515 appears cut-rate. Same-level giving is perpetuated. Some congregants may not want the church to have too much money, otherwise the leadership will just fritter it away on unnecessary items.

Thankfully, a growing number of congregations do not place the operating budget as the centerpiece of the pledge drive. An accurate budget is certainly important, but some members view each line item suspiciously, wondering why so much money needs to be spent for salaries, benefits, maintenance, and other costs. Can't we do all this for less? For many, the operating budget is a disincentive to give.

To be sure, some people wish to see the operating budget because they believe if X dollars are raised, then X programs will be implemented. This is their motivation to give, and the church should provide the figures. In my experience, though, the operating budget is not a wellspring of charitable giving for most members. They don't relate to a "pay the bills" mentality. Rather, they prefer being generous souls, and believe this adds to their innate goodness.

(On a related note, I do not recommend publishing monthly budget updates in the newsletter. Many people do not understand budgets, no matter how straightforward the numbers are presented. In many instances, there are confusing footnotes. Also, ongoing budget figures often show a deficit in pledges being paid, which can result in an attitude of fiscal uncertainty when one does not exist.)

New or exciting initiatives are an excellent way to stimulate giving in any congregation. But smaller congregations may have difficulty launching new efforts, given the staff and volunteer resources available. In these instances, a sense of urgency toward a desirable goal is an excellent alternative. I have found, however, that urgency is not a strong suit of most UU congregations. But I do believe that if an initiative is truly important, it will carry its own urgency.

For example, some smaller congregations have a particular vocation, such as "adopting" a school or other organization that serves people who are less fortunate. Such a vocation can be a motivation for creating a generous congregation, one that will encourage "second mile" giving, an attractive antidote to same-level giving.

Generosity should be a core UU value, at the heart of what it means to be a member or friend of a Unitarian Universalist congregation. Sadly, UUs rank among the least generous of American churchgoers. This is another tradition we should leave in the past.

## Doing away with the annual pledge drive

Making the annual pledge drive obsolete requires a new "mindset." It means shifting away from asking church members for money, and asking people to commit to a distinctive UU way of life.

Clergy and lay leaders who go this route will need a dose of courage in challenging themselves and their fellow church members to redefine the kind of lives they wish to lead. Theologically conservative churches routinely ask this of members. Liberal churches rarely do because they do not believe they offer a life-transforming experience, or have the authority to challenge the materialistic lifestyles of their members.

Numerous surveys indicate that churchgoers and non-churchgoers lead almost identical lives. If we live our lives no differently from our unchurched friends and neighbors, then what difference does the church make? If the church makes no difference in our day-to-day lives, then it's a social club and not a community of faith.

How do clergy, lay leaders, and we ourselves challenge the prevailing consumer culture? Here are some suggestions:

- I can't repeat often enough how important it is to encourage members and friends to reach the 5 to 10 percent giving level as soon as possible.

- UU congregations should give away the loose offering on Sundays, to organizations that live out our their values by assisting people in need. Churches that have gone this route have seen increases both in plate offerings and in the annual pledge drive. Committing the loose offering does not rob Peter to pay Paul.
- UU congregations need to be worthy recipients of people's charitable giving, and can gain this credibility by assigning at least 10 percent of their operating budgets to outreach, to those who are less fortunate. Outreach should be the first line item in the budget, and the first to be paid. All other items follow. Outreach should not come last, if there's anything left over. The outreach line item is in addition to denominational and district dues.
- Churches will do their members a great favor by offering classes in alternative ways of living. The Voluntary Simplicity movement has made it more socially acceptable for people to lead more simple lives, unencumbered by consumer goods. The church should also encourage its members toward debt-free living.
- Clergy might include references to simple lifestyles as an ongoing sermon topic. Many clergy may already live this life, not necessarily by choice, so this should be an easy topic on which to preach.
- Church members can be encouraged to purchase smaller, high-mileage automobiles and use public transportation whenever possible.
- Church members can be encouraged to purchase smaller, less extravagant homes. The architect Sarah Susanka is author of *The Not So Big House* series, which has brought a design-oriented perspective to helping people live creatively, comfortably, and stylishly in smaller homes. (www.susanka.com)
- Members can be encouraged to consider moving toward a vegetarian diet, as approximately five pounds of the world's resources are required to produce one pound of meat. This is a matter or stewardship of the earth on which we live.
- Climate scientists believe the key to a sustainable planet is people

who live simpler lives, closer to home. Will UUs consider this concept as a religious issue?

- Church members can be encouraged to view ostentatious displays of wealth as antithetical to what kind of people we are called to become.

Readers may be shocked! shocked! that the church would ask so much of them. But these recommendations aren't really a stretch. Observant Jews keep holy the Sabbath by doing no work, using no electricity, and spending no money for a full day each week.

I'm hoping UUs won't dismiss the above suggestions out of hand, but will consider a few items on the list. Doing so might be an interesting adventure, a lively change of pace. Besides, the things in life that hold great value require some effort. A strong, life-sustaining faith is no exception.

Leading a simpler life goes far beyond making personal choices. "Congregations of all faiths," according to Robert Wuthnow, "deplore the oppression of peoples, or decry the injustices to the unborn, or to gays and lesbians. But efforts to assist the downtrodden and disadvantaged and to speak for greater justice on their behalf can succeed only if middle class churchgoers are challenged in ways that have seldom been seen in recent decades."[8] UUs who lead lives that challenge the prevailing consumer culture will be the vanguard of progressive religion in our time.

Will UU clergy, lay leaders, and UUs themselves take up these challenges? In many faith traditions, the issue is not just the amount one gives to the church. The issue is using all the resources at one's command to craft lives of meaning and purpose. It's not just the five or ten percent we give to the church, but what we do with the remaining 90 to 95 percent, as well. Stewardship is all about a way of life.

UUs rank among the most well educated, successful Americans. What better legacy could we leave our children and grandchildren than belonging to a generous church; and that we are generous people in heart, spirit, and daily life.

Finally, I led a seminar at district gathering of about 150 UUs recently. I asked people in attendance to write down the answers to some questions I posed, and to hand in their answers. One of the questions was, "Would you make a sacrifice for a larger cause or a greater good?"

In reviewing their responses, I was extraordinarily heartened that 95 percent of respondents answered, "Yes, I would make a sacrifice for the greater good." Many of the responses contained marginal comments that said, "I wish my church asked this of me." I rest my case for increased giving and a distinctive UU way of life.

CHAPTER 7

# Five Helpful Heresies

Scripture, *n. The sacred books of our holy religion, as distinguished from the false and profane writings on which all other faiths are based.*
— Ambrose Bierce, *The Devil's Dictionary*

The word *heresy* gets a bad rap. When the word comes to mind, we might think of Michael Servetus, a 16th century heretic from our own ranks who was hanged in effigy by the Catholics and burned at the stake by order of the Protestant John Calvin. Heretics might also conjure up medieval scenarios involving people of various beliefs being tortured to recant their views.

Webster's defines the word *heresy* as, "An adherence to a religious opinion contrary to church doctrine." I suspect this definition is appealing to contemporary UUs, many of whom would willingly join the ranks of modern day heretics. Webster's also states that heresy and dissent often apply to the Roman Catholic Church, or to established Christian doctrine. Many UUs would be in sympathy with this definition as well.

But we need to consider a few heresies from within our own tradition. Doing so will mean some healthy soul-searching for clergy, lay leaders, and people in the pews alike.

## Heresy #1: UU ministers should get out of the intellectual stimulation business

The perennial surveys that ask why UUs attend Sunday services reveal that the #1 reason is intellectual stimulation. This finding is unfortunate. It perpetuates the belief that people come to church to be informed about religion, and do not perceive Unitarian Universalism as a faith that will change their lives in any substantive way. Thus, religion is of the mind and not the heart. Does this relegate modern day UUs to Ralph Waldo Emerson's Unitarians of the 19th century who he deemed, "Corpse cold intellectuals?" (UUs aren't the only ones who stand accused. Episcopalians are referred to as "God's frozen chosen.")

I am deeply touched by thought-provoking and well-preached sermons, and some UU ministers are extraordinarily gifted preachers. However,

> *intellectual stimulation from the pulpit is a gargantuan red herring that sidetracks the rightful purpose of UU congregations.*

Religious sentiment in the American public has shifted, and churchgoers view religious expression differently from years past. Robin Trebilcock, a minister and author of the book, *The Small Church at Large*, accurately conveys changing religious sentiment over the past few decades. He writes, "There has been a global cultural shift. That shift has been from a rational understanding of religion to a relational, experiential, and intuitive understanding."[1]

In Unitarian Universalism, this has been a shift away from the Unitarian tradition, with its emphasis on reason, logic, and individual self-sufficiency; toward a greater appreciation of Universalism, which concerns itself with the heart and soul, and for the great human family of which we are a part.

Since the 1970s, reason has become a diminishing factor in religious motivation. We can observe this trend in the declining memberships of the American Humanist Association and the American Ethical Society, institutions that are based on an intellectual approach to religion and faith. Many UUs may wish it otherwise, but the trends away from reason and intellect in religion are unmistakable.

In its place, growing numbers of churchgoers seek lives of greater meaning, purpose, and spiritual depth via religious sources and teachings. They search for hope, solace, and understanding in a world that appears evermore indeterminate. They wish for their children and grandchildren to have a solid faith that carries them through difficult times. They yearn to be part of a meaningful religious community that is different from the secular world they inhabit day to day. They want to experience religion in some way, not just learn about religion.

People are drawn to churches in times of joy and sorrow, and during life's various stages. They look for a church that offers a support group for new mothers, a program on getting out of debt, a class on parenting difficult teenagers, a divorce recovery class, or learning how to envision a new life as senior citizens. All these programs have religious underpinnings, and are intended to deepen one's faith. Some of these initiatives might fall into the intellectual stimulation category because people do learn things. But a more apt description is churches providing religious insight as people confront issues and challenges over the course of their lives.

Of course, some UUs congregations do these things, too. But Unitarian Universalism rarely views the congregation's primary purpose as assisting people along life's journey or deepening their faith. Rather, Unitarian Universalism has focused on the intellect, a method of information gathering that too often results in conversations about religion rather than defining a UU way of life by which people live in community.

The mind vs. the heart is not the only criteria by which to consider intellectual stimulation. Emphasizing the life of the mind does not bind people together with core values. In particular, sermons on secular topics that are similar to college lectures do not deepen a congregation's understanding of the faith, or the church's role in the larger society. Such sermons provide little that challenges members and friends to live differently than their friends or neighbors who have no interest in religion at all.

The minister's primary role is not to appear clever, erudite, and witty in the pulpit. Anthony Robinson addresses this in his book, *Transforming Congregational Culture*. He writes,

> *In my first ventures in the pulpit, I imagined my task to be something like that of an Op-Ed columnist. I was to comment on issues of the day, throw in a little Scripture, and scatter some pearls of wisdom in the direction of the waiting congregation. I might have gotten away with this but for my inchoate longing for something more and deeper.*
>
> *But with time I found that my task as a preacher was not simply to share what I had seen or heard in my encounter with God's story. It was to help people hear, see, discover, and be discovered for themselves. Instead of showing the slides, as it were, of my recent trip, it is acting as a guide for a river run of their own. When this kind of preaching happens, almost everyone gets wet. When the service ends, people do not walk out the door to go home for lunch and watch a football game. They walk out into a new world.*[2]

Robinson is exactly right. He is describing a method of preaching that leads congregants to an ever-deepening faith. This type of preaching is cumulative. It builds on fundamental values that parishioners hold in common and draws them together in a shared journey.

Some readers, particularly ministers, may wonder how to achieve this pinnacle of preaching on a regular basis. My answer is that over the long haul, it should be more profoundly satisfying to preach from the heart than from the head. I'm not advocating for sermons with little intellectual content. Rather, reminding congregants of core values they share in common will take an entire congregation deeper into the faith. Surely this is an alternative to searching, often frenetically, for new sermon topics week to week.

> *In my view, a faith that is cumulative in nature and deepens over time is a missing ingredient in Unitarian Universalism. UUs tend to view the church as coming through one great open door to religious freedom, rather than a series of doors to be opened over time.*

When I talk with UUs who don't attend services anymore, they often say they left the church not in anger, but because they had experienced everything Unitarian Universalism had to offer. They had heard a complete cycle of sermons. I've also heard UUs say regretfully, "I've been a member of this congregation for eight or nine years, and I'm not any more religious or spiritual now than when I joined."

Preaching from the head dates to centuries gone by, when the minister was the most highly educated person in the congregation. Many in the pews were illiterate. Obviously, this is no longer the case. Many congregants hold advanced degrees in specialized fields and are significantly better educated than the minister. Thus, for ministers, providing intellectual stimulation is eventually a losing proposition because the standard is so high. How many ministers can preach 30 or more stellar sermons on ever-changing topics year after year to a discerning and highly literate congregation?

Even when a minister has exceptional skills in the pulpit, the intellectual approach falls short. My former minister is keenly intelligent and extremely well read. He preaches brilliantly. He believes the perfect worship service is two hymns and a long sermon. In one series of sermons, he preached about the Five Pillars of Islam, the meaning of Jewish holidays, the Christian Right, the Ten Commandments, and contemporary humanism. Over six Sundays, he preached on five different subjects. I was greatly impressed.

While these were excellent sermons, the topics came so fast and furious that I could not keep up. Only 20 minutes devoted to subjects that would take a lifetime to comprehend and appreciate. While meeting every imaginable criterion for intellectual stimulation, these sermons were a veneer overlaying extraordinarily complex topics, somewhat like *Cliff's Notes*. I wish our congregation could have explored these issues in greater depth, or taken a few core concepts to study further, to strengthen and enhance the spiritual life of members.

These five excellent sermons had little long-term impact on the congregation's understanding of significant religious issues. I remember the topics but little more. I believe that sermons on ever-changing subjects keep parishioners at a minimalist level of faith. Intellectually-based sermons on secular concepts, compelling as they are at the time, often fail at the central task of deepening people's understanding of the ongoing role of religion in their lives. Such sermons do not reinforce congregants' awareness of their purpose and destiny.

I recall seeing a fellow congregant some years ago, a high-ranking faculty member at an Ivy League university, wearing a flowery apron while washing coffee cups after the Sunday service. I joked with him about his attire, and asked how he ended up at the kitchen sink. He laughed and said he gets more than enough intellectual stimulation at work, and that he comes to church for other reasons – to feel human, to remain humble, to serve in some capacity, to set an example, to become a better person. Isn't this what religion is all about?

Peter Gomes, minister of Harvard University's Memorial Church, echoes this sentiment when he writes, "Preaching deals with fundamental human themes such as identity, anxiety, desire, fear, greed, love, and death. Preaching that does not respond to the needs of the human condition is irrelevant, no matter how scholarly, pious, or eloquent it may be."[3]

I believe these primary religious values should provide ministers an extraordinary array of potential sermon topics that will last for many years to come.

### Heresy #2: Personal freedom and individual autonomy have outlived their usefulness as core values of Unitarian Universalism.

Unitarian Universalism is a faith of two minds. Our tradition embraces the doctrine of the autonomous, self-sufficient individual, yet UUs claim that building community is a high priority. Are conflicting goals possible?

Individualism and self-sufficiency reflect the "modern" era of the 1950s. During this time, modernism also included a sense of optimism and a belief in progress. Americans believed the world was in their hands, and with sufficient resolve, things would get sorted out.[4]

It is a vast understatement to say that we live in different times today. But as the years went by, Unitarian Universalism and liberal Protestantism tended to retain modernist values of individualism and personal autonomy, and now represent an era gone by. Religious progressives claim that individualism has co-opted the church. Today, individualism plays out in a consumer attitude of, "What's in it for me?" One key for UU congregations to envision a new tomorrow is to substitute a sense of service, as in, "What can I contribute?"

In perpetuating individualism, Unitarian Universalism has not challenged the superficiality of the consumer culture, nor presented alternatives. Rather, liberal congregations have conveyed an attitude that people can choose whatever beliefs they desire, like products in a department store. The Unitarian Universalist Association promotes this view in a sample mission statement that contains the phrase, "The right to make up one's own mind in religious beliefs."[5]

Successful religious movements put forth guidelines for daily living and help members become accountable for their spiritual maturity. They preach, teach, and help people understand timeless religious themes that will aid them in times of trouble and sorrow. They stand squarely against modernist notions that whatever an individual thinks is right.

I often remind UUs, sometimes facetiously and sometimes not, of our extraordinary ability never to do anything wrong. Since we don't believe in sin, no one ever commits any. We're all good people, you know. We don't need Yom Kippur, a day of atonement, like the Jews. We don't examine our consciences, like the Catholics. We don't concern ourselves with guilt over deeds done or undone, like the Christians. We don't require forgiveness, since we rarely, if ever, do harm to others in word or deed. We are just fine as we are. Our lives don't need to be changed. And we certainly don't view the church as having a say in these matters. We are autonomous. We possess individual freedom.

The concepts of self-sufficiency and self-determination can also create an attitude of superiority among UUs, that we are smarter than people of other faiths, especially Christians. This attitude is often reflected in hardened opinions among various segments of a congregation. Too often

I have sensed the stance, "I want what I want, and the church had better provide it." Sometimes threats of leaving the church or withholding financial support accompany this demand. Sometimes I think UUs could use a touch of humility.

I have also witnessed a tolerance of inappropriate behavior under the guise of individual freedom. A timely example is Internet "chat" groups that too often devolve into name-calling and people being "flamed" for their views. I have witnessed ministers being verbally scolded (and have been scolded myself, with accompanying finger-wagging) in reception lines following the Sunday service, because of remarks from the pulpit. As a footnote, I believe that inappropriate behavior among certain segments of the membership is only possible with the complicity of others.

An emphasis on individual freedom and personal autonomy can create unyielding views that act against creating a community of faith. I much prefer a way of life that encourages generosity of both the spirit and the pocketbook, the continual striving to become better people, the willingness to forgive, an acceptance of sacrifice for the greater good, and an eagerness to seek out new ways to serve the world. This is the religious life, one of richness and fullness. In my view, this tops personal autonomy any day.

## Heresy #3 The democratic process can consign a congregation to the past

"The use of the democratic process within our congregations" is one of Unitarian Universalism's deified Purposes and Principles. This phrase has been printed on thousands of posters, pamphlets, and fliers since the Purposes and Principles were formulated in the early 1980s. Most UUs could not recite more than one or two of the seven principles, but they are likely to recall the use of the democratic process.

A more helpful principle would be, "The use of the democratic process in small congregations and strong leadership in large congregations." It's an inverse proportion. The larger the congregation, the less effective the democratic process will be. Small congregations can function with a "town meeting" model of decision-making. Large congregations cannot. Let us consider the reasons why.

In smaller congregations, 125 or fewer at Sunday services, a larger percentage of the membership is likely to attend worship regularly, read the newsletter, and be reasonably informed about issues of the moment. More members are in the loop because smaller congregations emphasize friendship and community.

Smaller congregations tend to have easy-to-understand budgets and church life that is relatively uncomplicated. Routine decisions will affect most members in similar ways, and congregants believe they have a right to comment on issues proposed by clergy and lay leaders. This falls under the guise of, "All voices being heard." (The small church just described does not include those with sizable endowments, income-producing property, other complex financial circumstances, or a history of conflict.)

In many instances, open discussions and congregational votes can result in reasoned decisions. However, reaching the most suitable decision via congregational discussion and vote is not guaranteed. When presented with a choice between envisioning the future or preserving the past, congregations typically choose to preserve the past.

For example, new ventures or progressive measures that entail increased costs or some risk are infrequently approved by a majority vote. Sometimes, as noted earlier, votes on a particular issue end up close to a 50-50 split, which leaves half the congregation on the losing side. Votes sometimes break down along generational lines, which can polarize a congregation of older and younger members.

Thus, the use of the democratic process has potential drawbacks. Given the UU tendency for all voices to be heard, the democratic process can also leverage power to minority groups or to those who are the most vocal. Numerous UU congregations have seen plans for the future curtailed because of views held by fewer than 10 percent of the membership. An analogy is the old-fashioned steam engine train in cowboy movies that has an emergency cord running through the cars. One person anywhere on board can yank that cord and stop the entire train and all its passengers.

Few churches are immune from segments of the congregation who wish to preserve the status quo. Clergy and lay leaders should note the presence of groups that can be described by the acronym MOVE – Members Opposed to Virtually Everything. Such groups often employ the democratic process to enforce their views. In my experience, no amount of reason or explanation is sufficient to satisfy those who stand solidly against proposed change that the majority supports.

Smaller congregations may be habituated to the democratic process through custom and tradition. Churches of between 125 and 250 at

Sunday worship may have to work with a hybrid model, allowing congregational input but with the leadership eventually making a final decision. This is tricky territory. I believe readers will find the chapter on leadership helpful in this regard.

But a vocal minority should not be permitted to stall large congregations, those with 250 or more at Sunday worship, by wielding an ill-defined notion of the democratic process.

An effective formula for decision-making in large congregations is the approval of 25 percent of the average Sunday worship attendance. (This formula applies to most congregational decisions. Exceptions include conducting a capital campaign, calling a new minister, or some controversial issue.)

For example, consider a UU congregation with a membership of 625, whose Sunday attendance is 300. Twenty-five percent of 300 in attendance is 75 members, or about 12 percent of the total membership. Is it possible for a church to forge ahead on most initiatives when 88 percent of the membership may not have a say in the matter?

Let's take a closer look at that 88 percent of the membership. Since 300 members attend services regularly, this means 325 members do not. Those who are absent are unlikely to read the newsletter regularly, and may know little about the subject at hand. They cannot be assumed to hold informed opinions. Many of these members may also be low-level donors, or non-donors. Is collecting uninformed opinions from the least knowledgeable group of true value? Should the least informed and least committed members be the most influential regarding decisions about the congregation's future? This makes no sense whatsoever.

Continuing our analysis, in most congregations about 25 percent of the membership is truly knowledgeable about current issues because they commit the most time, effort, and money to the enterprise. One need merely look at the church's donor list to confirm this observation. These are the voices that matter. In our sample congregation, 25 percent of the 625-member church totals 155 people. Coincidently, about that same number of people is likely to attend the church's annual meeting, or a meeting to vote on some issue or another.

To complete the math, in a meeting of approximately 150 people where decisions are to be made, the aforementioned 75 people who represent 25 percent of the average Sunday attendance almost constitute a majority. These 75 members will include the most respected church members who have the congregation's best interests at heart. Chances are that others present will support their views. If a vote is taken, lo and behold, the church has utilized the democratic process because the decision to move forward was made by a majority of those who were present and are the most committed to the church. This is eminently sensible.

Let's consider another scenario. I'm familiar with a church that wished to sell its current building and purchase a larger structure. During the discussions that ensued, two minority groups emerged. One group wanted to mull over the possibility of a different site, and the other wanted to remain in the current building.

The leadership of this congregation made a very wise decision. They encouraged both groups to develop their views, and guaranteed their voices would be heard. *But the ground rule was that only constructive alternatives would be considered. Minority groups were not permitted to sit idly on the sidelines and criticize the process in place.* In the end, the congregational vote was 99 percent to follow the original plan.

The issue is not the democratic process per se. Rather, the issue is how the democratic process can be effectively utilized to help progressive, forward-thinking leaders envision a new tomorrow. The democratic process should not be used as a cudgel by minority groups to bring a congregation of any size to a standstill.

## Heresy #4 The Vision Thing

If your congregation's mission or vision statement contains phrases like inward journeys toward truth, the free exchange of ideas, intellectual freedom, creating beauty, honoring the democratic process, ennobling harmony, or free inquiry, that statement holds little value.

The UUA's 98-page publication, *Vision, Mission, and Covenant: Creating a Future Together,* will guarantee that your congregation ends up with a characterless statement of this ilk.[6]

From a pessimistic perspective, this doesn't matter because most UUs could not recite their congregation's mission statement anyway. Most statements are rambling and wordy, formulated by committees, and are not internalized by either clergy or congregants. I recall meeting with the Vision Committee of a UU congregation shortly after a yearlong process to devise a new vision statement. Their statement fit the description above.

I offered $20 to any member of the committee who could recite the new statement without error. None could.

However, the language of a congregation's mission or vision statement is vitally important if that congregation genuinely wishes to live out its call to ministry. A mission statement reveals the nature and character of that congregation, its place in the world, and what the future might hold.

Let's contrast the vision phrases above with an example from another faith tradition. This mission statement is from the Prince of Peace Lutheran Church in Minnesota. It reads, "You will be cared for, and will be called upon to care for others." That's it. Fourteen words. That mission statement is printed on just about every piece of paper that goes out the door. Those 14 words guide everything this 9,000-member congregation does.

The meaning of this alluring statement has many facets. It is welcoming to all, regardless of station in life. It is non-theological, and applies to people of many beliefs. It is outward-oriented, toward service to others. It suggests motion, that members will not merely take up residence. It implies action, that important work needs to be done. It is broad in perspective, signifying many ways to serve. It is easy to remember, to incorporate into one's life, and to share with others.

This congregation lives its vision each day because the mission statement is ever-present and oft repeated. This church measures its effectiveness by how its members travel the distance between being served and serving others. This is the journey upon which they are embarked. It's all about movement. It is a journey on which people of all ages can travel; a journey that is lifelong, timeless in its message of love, hope, and promise. This church's purpose could not be clearer. UU churches should be so fortunate.

## Heresy #5 Conducting a congregational survey is a dreadful idea

A congregational survey is a first cousin of the democratic process and suffers the same limitations. Surveys often gather uninformed opinions from those who know little about congregational life and the issues at hand.

Anonymous surveys, often the preferred method, are especially pernicious because they result in a disproportionate number of responses from those who are disgruntled. A survey is a tailor-made soapbox for this crowd.

Anonymous surveys do not distinguish opinions from the most dedicated and least dedicated members. Thus, the views of church members who attend services regularly, give generously, and fulfill leadership roles are equal to those who rarely show up, give little, and know the least about the dynamics of the congregation. Surveys also tend to turn out more responses from those who are opposed to new ideas.

Yet, the congregational survey is well entrenched in UU life, like kudzu in Southern states. If my argument does not dissuade your congregation from conducting a survey, the results will be infinitely more beneficial if you ask respondents for their names, how often they attend Sunday services, if they have held a leadership role in recent years, and the amount of their current pledge. This information will give credit where credit is due. Otherwise, anonymous surveys are akin to giving credibility to the writers of anonymous letters.

In my experience, not much is learned from congregational surveys anyway. The most common survey is taken when a church conducts the search for a new minister. Supposedly, results from the survey will help define the church, its membership, and what congregants are looking for in that new minister.

I've seen dozens of these surveys and the results are remarkably similar. About half the members are over 50 years of age, and have been around for more than 25 years. About 60 percent are humanist. Good preaching is always the #1 goal that is sought in the new minister. It only takes a few moments to skim survey results to determine that little content is truly meaningful. (Thankfully, the UUA has asked churches other questions that are more probing, such as the experience of the previous minister, the level of pledging, and the most significant issue the congregation is facing.)

When used in the search process, congregational surveys attempt to put the church's best foot forward, and do not reveal inherent shortcomings. For example, one UU minister was called to a church in which the current board chair was the seventh choice and had almost no involvement in congregational life. The board was extremely weak, most committees were ineffective, and the membership committee had not had a chair for two years. None of this was revealed in the survey results. The church presented itself as healthy, and the minister was subjected to a rude awakening early on. She believed she had been deceived by the congregational survey in particular.

Finally, a caveat to settled ministers. The phrase, "congregational survey" should strike dismay in their hearts because a survey is often the first step in removing the minister. A survey is a wolf in sheep's clothing. It is often presented as, "It's time we ask members how the church is doing, how it's meeting their needs," or, "We need to make sure we understand the membership's real concerns." Be forewarned. If you hear this recommendation from credible leaders or influential members, it may already be too late.

I don't have a suggestion for an alternative to the congregational survey. In my experience, a congregation that understands and lives out its purpose doesn't need one.

AFTERWORD

# My Plea to Unitarian Universalism

Walter Bruggeman is a man whose words can change your life. Bruggeman is a renowned Old Testament scholar, the author of 58 books and hundreds of articles about Scripture and the contemporary church. I had the privilege of hearing him speak recently.

Bruggeman believes that people frequently come to church with feelings of loneliness, despair, uncertainty, and unresolved anger. They attempt to face life's challenges with honesty and integrity, but may feel inadequate to the task. They are dismayed at seeing greed and evil in the world triumph. They believe their feelings need to be acknowledged, to be honored.

What they often find is a church that offers up timid prayers and anemic meditations. They hear, "Be still before the mystery of life," on Sunday morning. At memorial services they hear the soothing words of the 23rd Psalm, "He maketh me lie down in green pastures." A more appropriate reading that reflects people's raw emotions would be the 22nd Psalm, "My God, My God, why hast thou forsaken me?"

"Pain needs to be brought to speech," Bruggeman stated forcefully, "in order for people to be made truly whole, to experience the depth and meaning of the religious life. But when people come to church they are told they shouldn't harbor these feelings, to wish them away."

UU congregations need a strong enough God, however defined, to handle the world's most troubling concerns. Failing to define such a God limits the emotional repertoire that people in community can and should experience together.

I confess that I have conflicting thoughts that seem to have no outlet in Unitarian Universalism. Sometimes I go to church feeling lonely and doubtful, but I dutifully take my place in the pew, maintain an outward decorum, sit and listen quietly. I participate in chitchat during the coffee hour. I am nice. But I am not genuine. I come away more troubled than when I arrived.

Writers far more insightful than I have taken liberal religion to task for standing in the wings while others claim center stage – faiths that preach intolerance, strident voices in the media that foster rage and resentment, the incessant drumbeat of advertising that advocates mindless consumerism, television and movies that are disturbingly violent. Brueggeman says that liberal churches do not possess the potent language required to thwart the destructive effects of contemporary society. It makes me wish we had a heavy-duty God.

Appendix A

# Recommended Books

Creating a summary of books on the spiritual life is a challenge. Thousands of books have been written on the subject. Below are a few suggestions from mostly contemporary authors. Some are Christian-oriented, but all are chosen for their extremely insightful views in regard to broad religious themes.

## Nonfiction

Gordon Atkinson: *RealLivePreacher.com*

Frederick Buechner: *Listening to Your Life: Daily Meditations*

Barbara Brown Taylor: *Leaving Church: A Memoir of Faith*

Thomas Merton: *Conjectures of a Guilty Bystander*

Kathleen Norris: *Dakota: A Spiritual Geography* and *The Cloister Walk*

Parker J. Palmer: *Let Your Life Speak: Listening for the Voice of Vocation*

Marcus Borg: *Jesus: Uncovering the Life, Teachings, and Relevance of a Religious Revolutionary*

Thomas Moore: *Care of the Soul: A Guide for Cultivating Depth* and *Sacredness in Everyday Life*

Reinhold Niebuhr: *Leaves from the Notebook of a Tamed Cynic*

Jim Wallis: *The Great Awakening: Reviving Faith and Politics in a Post-Religious Right America*

Bart D. Ehrman: *God's Problem: How the Bible Fails to Answer Our Most Important Question - Why We Suffer*

Richard J. Foster: *Celebration of Discipline: The Path to Spiritual Growth*

Henri J.M. Nouwen: *Spiritual Direction: Wisdom for the Long Walk of Faith;* or *Life of the Beloved: Spiritual Living in a Secular World;* or *The Dance of Faith: Weaving Sorrows and Blessings Into One Joyful Step.*

Diana Butler Bass: *Christianity for the Rest of Us*

John Baillie: *A Diary of Private Prayer*

Augustine: *Confessions*

Peter J. Gomes: *Strength for the Journey* and *The Good Life*

Walter Bruggeman: *The Prophetic Imagination* and *Prayers for a Privileged People*

Robert B. Stewart: *The Future of Atheism*

Damien Keown: *Buddhism: A Short Introduction*

John L. Esposito. *What Everyone Needs to Know About Islam*

Phyllis Tickle: *The Divine Hours*

Gene Robinson: *In the Eye of the Storm*

Julian of Norwich: *Showings*

Philip Jacob Spener: *Pia Desideria*

Richard Lischer: *Open Secrets*

## Fiction

Elizabeth Strout: *Abide With Me*

Marilynne Robinson: *Gilead*

Sinclair Lewis: *Elmer Gantry*

Sheri Reynolds: *The Rapture of Canaan*

Alfred Alcorn: *Vestments*

# References


**Introduction**

1. Thom S. Rainer and Eric Geiger, *Simple Church* (Nashville, TN. B&H Publishing Group, 2008), 65.
2. Edward H. Hammett, *Reaching People Under 40 While Keeping People over 60* (St. Louis, MO, 2007), introduction.
3. Gordon MacDonald, *Who Stole My Church?* (Nashville, TN. Thomas Nelson Press, 2007)

**Chapter One**

1. Jim Wallis, God's Politics: *A New Vision for Faith and Politics in America* (San Francisco, CA. HarperCollins, 2005) introduction.
2. Rev. William Murry, from a sermon delivered in New York, October 27, 2002.

**Chapter Two**

1. Lyle Schaller, *44 Steps Up Off the Plateau* (Nashville, TN. Abingdon Press, 1993), 84.
2. Anthony Robinson, *What's Theology Got to Do With It?* (Herndon, VA. The Alban Institute, 2006), 25.
3. Paul Nixon, *I Refuse to Lead a Dying Church* (Cleveland, OH. The Pilgrim Press, 2006), 57.
4. Robinson, *What's Theology Got to Do With It?*, 27.
5. Jim Henderson and Matt Casper, *Jim and Casper Go to Church* (Carol Stream, IL. Tyndale House Publishers, 2007), xi.
6. Alexandra Alter, "The Mystery Worshiper," *The Wall Street Journal*, October 10, 2008, page W1.

7. April Dembosky, "Finding Jesus on Facebook, and Putting Young People in the Pews," *The New York Times*, October 26, 2008, 31.

8. Edward H. Hammond, *Reaching People Under 40 While Keeping People Over 60*, 32.

9. Lyle Schaller, *44 Ways to Increase Church Attendance* (Nashville, TN. Abingdon Press, 1988), 21.

10. Lyle Schaller, *44 Steps Up Off the Plateau*, 84-87.

**Chapter Three**

1-2 Lyle Schaller's many books are published by Abingdon Press, Nashville, TN.

3. Nixon, *I Refuse to Lead a Dying Church*, 17-18

4. Nixon, 19.

5. Jeffrey E. Greenway, *Make Room to Grow: Transform the Church Without Killing the Congregation* (Nashville, TN. Abingdon Press, 2007), 1.

6. Anthony Robinson, *Transforming Congregational Culture* (Grand Rapids, MI. William B. Eerdmans Publishing Company, 2003), 21-22.

**Chapter Four**

1. Gordon Atkinson, *RealLivePreacher.com* (Grand Rapids, MI. William B. Eerdman's Publishing Company, 2004), 12.

**Chapter Five**

1. Marilynne Robinson, *Gilead* (New York, NY. Farrar, Straus, and Giroux, 2004), 47.

2. Julie-Ann Silberman-Bunn, *The Satisfaction Business, in Living A Call: Ministers and Congregations Together* (Tulsa, OK. Jenkin Lloyd Jones Press, 2006), 11.

3. Paul Wilkes, *Excellent Protestant Congregations* (Louisville, KY. Westminster John Knox Press, 2001), 65.

4. "Building Relationships," *The Christian Century Magazine*, May 20, 2008, pp 10-11.

5. Robinson, *Transforming Congregational Culture*, 80.

6. Rainer and Geiger, *Simple Church*, 103.
7. Michael Durall, *The Almost Church: Redefining Unitarian Universal* (Tulsa, OK. Jenkin Lloyd Jones Press, 2004), 7.
8. James Fowler, *Stages of Faith* (New York, NY. Harper and Row, 1981)
9. Kathleen Norris, *Dakota: A Spiritual Geography* (New York, NY. Houghton Mifflin, 1993), 23.

**Chapter Six**

1. Robert Wuthnow, *The Crisis in the Churches: Spiritual Malaise, Fiscal Woe* (New York, NY. Oxford University Press, 1999), 230.
2. Anthony Robinson, *Transforming Congregational Culture*, 89.
3. Walter Bruggeman, *Mandate to Difference* (Louisville, KY. Westminster John Knox Press, 2007), 5.
4. Robert Wuthnow, *Christianity in the 21st Century: Reflections on the Challenges Ahead* (New York, NY. Oxford University Press, 1993), 134.
5. Ibid, 193.
6. Stanley Haurewaus and William Willimon, *Resident Aliens: A Provocative Assessment of Culture and Ministry for People Who Know Something is Wrong* (Nashville, TN. Abingdon Press, 1989), 32.
7. *AARP Bulletin*, Washington, DC. September 2008, page 3.
8. Wuthnow, *The Crisis in the Churches*, 6-7.

**Chapter Seven**

1. Robin Trebilcock, "Horse Whisperer Evangelism," *Net Results Magazine*, November-December 2007, 16.
2. Anthony Robinson, *Transforming Congregational Culture*, 43.
3. Peter Gomes, *Strength for the Journey* (San Francisco, CA. Harper-Collins, 2003), xiv.
4. Anthony Robinson, *What's Theology Got to do With It?*, 11-13
5. *Vision, Mission, and Covenant: Creating a Future Together*, at www.uua.org
6. Ibid, p. 73.